D0940450

How to be your BEST at EVERYTHING ...
EVERY TIME!

LIVING

IMPOSSIBLE

DREAMS

A 7-Step Blueprint to help you break free from limiting beliefs that have chained you down, so you can achieve greatness in all areas of your life.

Freddy Behin, MD

This book is available in the following formats:

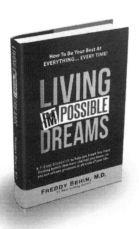

Paperback
Hardcover
eBook
Audio Book

To purchase any of these formats please visit:

www.LivingImpossibleDreams.com

COPYRIGHT

SIMA PUBLISHING
22815 Ventura Blvd Suite 500
Woodland Hills, CA 91364

Copyright © 2017 by **Freddy Behin**

All rights reserved.

No part of this publication including diagrams, images and photos may be reproduced, distributed, or transmitted in any form or by any means, including photocopying, recording, or other electronic or mechanical methods, without the prior written permission of the publisher, except in the case of brief quotations embodied in critical reviews and certain other noncommercial uses permitted by United States of America copyright law.

Printed in the United States of America

Library of Congress Cataloging-in-Publication Data available.

1st Edition (v4.1)

ISBN: 978-0-9985979-1-1 (Paperback)
ISBN: 978-0-9985979-2-8 (Hardcover)
ISBN: 978-0-9985979-0-4 (E-book)
ISBN: 978-0-9985979-3-5 (Audio book)
ASIN: B0195YIS96

For contact information please visit:
www.LivingImpossibleDreams.com

DEDICATION

This book is dedicated to my mom and dad.

My mom for always being a giving and patient woman, a supportive woman and the inspiration of my life, who had many skill sets and the ability to see the details in things that many around her could never see. A woman who taught me the selfless art of compassion and love. My mother, who taught me how to strive for perfection, thank you.

My dad, who I always appreciated his being tough to please. A hard working, stubborn and proud man who always protected his emotions inside for no one to see. In his own way, he pushed me to achieve success.

My parents could have not possibly been more different in their ways; but they both gave me values and distinctions.

Thank you both for inadvertently helping me build my mindset and the hunger for more.

SPECIAL THANKS

Special thanks to Dr. Barbara Rembiesa for her editing efforts and her support in organizing this book. She is a woman with a huge heart for serving humanity and a tenacious unbreakable spirit.

I would also like to thank Kimberly Chow for her support in critiquing my work and always finding some spelling errors despite my tedious efforts to not make them.

FOREWORD

There are very few people we meet in life that have all personal aspirations and goals set at a young age. I have known Dr. Freddy Behin for almost 25 years as his former gymnastics coach. Presently as the top authority and the world's chief men's Olympic gymnastics judge, I meet top athletes and judges from around the world in many sports. No one I have met has the drive and determination of Freddy.

Before attending UCLA, he already was on the road to great accomplishments. Freddy was not just satisfied competing as a World Championship level gymnast; he also wanted to be original. Gymnasts worldwide strive to have a new skill named after them in the rule book of gymnastics, the Code of Points.

This gives them an everlasting legacy in the sport. Freddy accomplished this prior to starting his collegiate gymnastics career at legendary UCLA. He had a skill named after him on the Rings at the World Championships, bringing international attention.

I was always concerned about Freddy attempting to compete for UCLA and the world stage, while studying to become a future medical doctor. Most other high achieving people would have found this impossible, but Freddy never wavered once after this goal was set. Persistence and unrelenting effort are attributes which have guided his success. He also has the ability to rebound quickly from any setback, a trait matched by the most effective people in the world.

His motivation and resilience were an inspiration for all around him, especially the athletes, coaches, and judges surrounding him in the past. I regularly tell young gymnasts, do not wait for your coach to push you, you need to push the coach. Freddy inspired this phrase, which I regularly tell Olympians eyeing the Olympic Games. This book only scratches the surface of what can be learned from Dr. Freddy Behin, offering unselfish lessons about living life to the fullest.

Steve Butcher

World's Chief Men's Olympic Gymnastics Judge
Coach of Olympians

TESTIMONIALS

"I wanted to take a moment to introduce you to a very respected colleague and friend of mine, Dr. Freddy Behin, who rose from humble beginnings to achieve not only one, but many of his impossible dreams.

Even more than his incredible high-achieving drive, what sets him apart is his integrity, his huge heart, and the way he loves to help the people around him. Freddy is one of those individuals who will have an impact on your life one way or another.

I hope that you get the chance to work with Freddy, and let him guide you through his magic!"

Brian Tracy

Entrepreneur, Professional Speaker, Best Selling Author & Success Expert

"Impossible is a word used by those who are afraid of themselves. 'Impossible' is a concept that keeps the masses asleep and controllable. Impossible is a conductor that synchronizes insecurities to work together as one. Freddy Behin doesn't speak that word, understand that concept, or take direction from that conductor."

Dr. Sean Stephenson

Author of "Get Off Your 'BUT': How to end self-sabotage and stand up for yourself"

"For Dr. Freddy Behin no problem is too big. I met Freddy while doing residency in Plastic Surgery at UMDNJ. While treating patients, he was writing a software and designing equipment to improve patient care. He was doing that while he was pulling in double shifts at the hospital as well as studying for his board exams and publishing his 'Demystifying Z-Plasty' article. Did I mention he was running a business back in California as well?

Years later after our initial encounter working as physicians when he learned about our need to assist patients in Philippines, very selflessly, he volunteered and dropped anything else to come and help change lives. This level of altruism and idealism is very rare in individuals who have already paved their life. Freddy has a big heart for helping people around him and I have seen his infectious personality to connect with people throughout the years. Freddy has a tenacious drive and I have seen him crush obstacles as they come his way. I am very excited that he will be sharing some of his tricks with you."

Michael M. Omidi, MD FACS

Plastic & Reconstructive Surgeon
Chief of Medical Staff NMP - No More Poverty

"Upon first meeting Freddy I immediately recognized his infectious personality. His big smile and warm demeanor had an illuminating kindness that was lit with giving, genuine love. Imagine for a moment that spending 3 days with someone so incredible who has the ability to affect hundreds, if not thousands of people for many years to come.

In this book, Freddy will walk us through a foolproof system to take ourselves to the next level. Whether it is training for a world championship or preparing to save a life through delicate surgery, Freddy has trained his mind, body, and soul to ensure his actions create the results and reputation of a world-class individual.

Continuing his servitude towards humanity, Freddy has decided to share the necessary skills and attributes to help you make a true difference in the world.

Freddy has created around himself a world that has been molded by the positive actions he has taken in life and will leave a legacy that will imprint itself on the lives and hearts of everyone he has touched.

Forge your legacy. Leave your mark on the world."

Dr. Barbara Rembiesa, D.Litt

CEO & President IAITAM, Inc.

"Years from now you will be more disappointed
by the things you didn't do
than by the things you did do."

- Mark Twain

"Time won't wait for you!
You must do all the things that you want to do
and live your dreams NOW.
When NOW would be a great time to get started?"

- Freddy Behin

TABLE OF CONTENTS

CHAPTER
1

Introduction

INTRODUCTION

LIMITING BELIEF

Have you ever wondered why you may enjoy some activities and dislike others? What about how you enjoy one thing but loathe something else? How about beliefs? What makes you believe you can or cannot do something? Why do you doubt yourself?

On the surface it seems we – as humans – are all pre-programmed to accept these limitations. Somehow, we go through life thinking that "it is the way it is" and that is a good enough response to justify how we feel. This feeling is often associated with challenges that seem insurmountable. That the problem is so big or so complicated that it is difficult to even understand where to begin, and we come to terms with it.

We come to terms with identifying ourselves as either being talented, or not; gifted, or not. We are either fortunate or unfortunate and there is no middle ground.

But you know who doesn't think that way? Do you know the people who surround us every day that are not limited by anything other than their imagination? Children. When children are asked "What do you want to be when you grow up?" you almost never hear a child giving an excuse or a personal limitation story explaining why they cannot do something. They simply dream, and often dream big! In dreaming the big dream they have no doubt that what they dream will one day be a reality. Their faces light up and they can be heard speaking with the truest of conviction that their future will be exactly as they have dreamt it.

Rarely however do we find adults who are living the dreams they had as a child. Usually, you will not find an adult who can actually say "I am exactly where I thought I would be when I was younger." Instead, when you ask the adult why they're not living their childhood or current dreams you will get incredibly convincing stories about why those dreams were simply unrealistic.

Sometimes they tell you that they simply did not have the right resources such as talent, ability, exposure, connections, and so on. Many times you get the story of obstacles that were placed in front of them or people who were at fault. The underlying message that all those stories have in common is that it was not in my power and ultimately not my fault.

My question is; what happened? What happened to us? Why did we lose the ability to dream and the ability to believe in our own potential? What are the causes that make us give up on our dreams? These are the same dreams that once fueled our lives and consumed our every waking moment.

What occurred was a reality shift. At some point in our lives our reality shifted and in turn, our identity shifted with it. We make a conscious decision that limitations exist or worse, that we ourselves have limitations. As inconsequential as this concept may seem, the problem arises when we view ourselves through the inability to accomplish something. These limitations actually increase the longer we remain in this mindset. So we begin to spread out and find new limitations and new reasons to dismiss our failure or our inability to try. Not only do we stop dreaming but we put boundaries on our dreams. Now even a dream will have a limitation. Those boundaries then fence us in with feelings of inadequacy and doubt until they stop us from experiencing our dreams and our goals altogether.

After all, if you set low expectations and low standards for yourself, you are less likely to fail. This is especially true if you don't try. Often, we fail to try because we believe that what has been imagined is an impossible dream in the first place.

For far too many of us, we have given up on our long forgotten dreams. We have created a series of very convincing and compelling reasons to justify why we have given up. This has led many of us to believe that our inability to achieve our dreams is simply not our fault. Obviously, this is another lie that we tell ourselves.

These excuses are simply defense mechanisms that we utilize to shield ourselves from the ultimate fear which all humans live with. Regardless of gender, race, ethnicity, culture, etc. all humans share the same fear:

Fear of not being good enough!

We fear that if we are not good enough then we are not worthy enough. That lack of self-worth manifests itself as a fear that we are undeserving of love. As a result, so many people who have a low self-worth seek out love from sources they feel they deserve. Unfortunately, these are often self-destructive and manifest themselves as addiction, negative attention-seeking, and self-deprecation.

A very select few are motivated by this fear and it pushes those people to achieve greatness. For the majority however, this fear of failure limits us from achieving greatness at all. In the following chapters, you will learn about the limitations and how to conquer them. You will also learn specific tools that will help you to achieve any goal you set your mind to.

Starting right here, and right now, we will go on a journey together to rediscover what it was like to dream as a child, to play until we win and live a life full of potential without the limitations of the adult mind.

Let me ask you some questions:

- Do you remember the first time you gave up on a dream? This would be the impossible dream that seemed insurmountable but excited you to the core.
- Do you remember when you first agreed with other people when they vocalized limiting concepts about you?

You see, I too was relentlessly challenged by those same negative voices that said "it's not possible." I knew however, that if there was at least a one in a million chance, I could figure out how to achieve success. I also knew that this was not going to be my last time battling those negative voices so I knew that I had to find a way to make my success repeatable.

So, I created a Blueprint that has become the key to it all. I have used this Blueprint repeatedly throughout my life and it has helped me to defy insurmountable odds and live out my own impossible dreams:

- I dreamed of becoming a world-class gymnast competing at the Gymnastics World Championship while I was a starting gymnast at UCLA
- I dreamed of leaving a legacy on the sport, to invent my own gymnastics strength move on the gymnastic rings that was so spectacular and so difficult that I would be the only gymnast in global history to successfully execute it during competition

- I dreamed of becoming a Medical Doctor when everyone I knew within the medical community doubted that I would even be accepted into medical school

- I dreamed of being able to communicate multiple languages fluently without an accent despite the language department teachers in high school telling me I did not have any talent for linguistics

- I dreamed of being a software developer, developing computer code and programming modeling software that could radically simplify what was used by software researchers and cardiologists during their research for the first artificial pacemaker and assisting them in understanding electrical chaos in cardiac fibrillation and re-entering spiral waves in diseased hearts

- I dreamed of having a successful gymnastics gym that took an alternative approach allowing all children to have a fair opportunity to learn and enjoy the sport with dignity and fun. An approach different to the way the gymnastics community did things even though I was told my business model would fail

- I dreamed of becoming a successful entrepreneur and leader and to become a top-results success coach and speaker thus helping other people live a fulfilling life and achieve their wildest dreams as I have

I have always done whatever it takes to figure out what works and now I am finally ready to share the secrets of my Blueprint that I created with you. The steps in my Blueprint may seem familiar and even simple at first glance but make no mistake, I have refined this process and have filled each step in this book with stories and strategies that will help you.

We need to agree on a ground rule right here and right now. If you are reading this book, you have already demonstrated that you are a person who is growth oriented. You are a person who takes action. Our ground rule is that you will keep an open mind – and even if you believe you may have heard any of the concepts before – to read and listen to it with a fresh pair of eyes and ears. Most importantly learn as if you have to teach it to someone you love whose life will change because of you. Is that a deal? OK then, let us get started.

My Blueprint has seven steps:

1. **Mindset** – You will learn a new way to view yourself, your ability and visualize your future success.

2. **Desire** – The fuel to keep you going when everyone else stops and we will discuss strategies to make it fun.

3. **Decision** – I will show you how I leverage discipline and responsibility to bust through any and all obstacles. Your decisions shape your future.

4. **Planning** – You will learn how to map out success by being clear about your outcome and goals. Exploring a variety of ways to get to your outcomes, while anticipating roadblocks and setback along the way.

5. **Preparation** – This is the psychology and your belief system around your outcome. This allows you to take the right steps at the right time and see results efficiently, while minimizing risk.

6. **Work** – Success comes through hard work but working smarter and focusing on areas that maximize results is key.

7. **Evaluate** – Learn how to fine-tune your actions and identify where to make the required changes when challenges present themselves.

I will lead you through my step-by-step proven process for helping people just like yourself achieve and live their own *im*possible dreams.

I am honored to share my Blueprint with you. It has been the secret to my success and I am excited to guide you through achieving your own *im*possible dreams!

Bonus Material
Infographic of the entire process of the blueprint in this book.

Download:
www.LivingImpossibleDreams.com/bonus/blueprint

BLUEPRINT

CHAPTER
2

BECOMING A WORLD CLASS ATHLETE

MY STORY

The excitement sets in as I get closer to the arena for the competition. I could feel it deep, in every fiber of my being, that the world stage was getting nearer and that all eyes in the gymnastics world were about to descend on this very spot. I was on a large tour bus with several other athletes who all shared my same expression of anticipation. As we were being bused in from the hotel into the arena I took the opportunity to look around at the people I was sharing my bus with and quickly recognized many of the athletes. Some of these athletes were currently the stars in the world arena and others present as coaches who were my heroes and idols as a young athlete growing up and helped drive my passion for gymnastics.

As the bus pulled up to the arena I quickly gathered my training bag and got off the bus. Alongside all the other athletes, I walked towards the training facility. We were three short days away from the 1996 Gymnastics Championships.

It was a weird feeling listening to the strange symphony that filled the air. There must have been at least six different countries represented on this tour bus and each country had four to five people speaking in their native language. As we walked through the rear entrance for the stadium and training center, we went through tunnels where the languages echoed and blended into an incoherent sound that is as unforgettable as it was unique. The strangest part however was when everyone unanimously fell silent. Everyone was mesmerized by the giant stadium and arena that was in front of them. The exact arena where in 3 days we would all be performing what we have spent years training for. Although all the seats in this ten thousand seat stadium were empty I could somehow hear and see the audience in those seats.

While observing my surroundings I could not help but notice a large banner on the side railing which read "Welcome to the Gymnastics World Championships." As my eyes surveyed each letter and the reality of the situation began to sink in I felt chills running down my arms and spine. My body was overwhelmed with excitement and nervous anticipation knowing that I had indeed "made it". I was actually inside the arena where the best in the world would compete. I was here in the arena where the World Championships would be held and I would compete against the best gymnasts from around the globe and it is exactly the way I played it out in my mind hundreds of times.

It appeared as if there was no ceiling to the stadium and it had seating for over twenty-thousand people. All the equipment was brand new and came together seamlessly. The smell of a gymnastics arena covered in new vinyl mats, wooden bars, chalk, and leather creates an unmistakable smell that is immediately recognizable.

I look to my left and right and see my Dad and my coach with me. They too are mesmerized by the massive stadium and are taking in the experience.

I was snapped out of my wonderment by a smiling man who tapped me on the shoulder and said "Sir, we must go to the registration booth. Please, follow me." Each country had one or two helpers and guides as personal assistants for the entire competition. My helper was Carlos and he always greeted me with a warm smile.

We made our way to the registration booth where the entire delegation including athletes, coaches, and trainers received their official badge. This badge allowed everyone to enter and leave the secured arena as well as the training center.

After getting my badge, Carlos and I went to the locker room to get geared up and ready for a practice run on these newly installed equipment. Taking a short moment to catch my breath and allow the reality of everything to set in I got dressed and headed out into the arena. My practice session included a light run, a couple bounces as well as stretching my muscles. Being warmed up and limber is important for any athlete but especially important for a gymnast as we are doing techniques that require an immense amount of strength and flexibility.

I was not alone in my warm-up session. All the athletes for the event had convened to the arena to begin their preparations. We were all busy and incredibly focused on our specific tasks. We each had a purpose for being there and were dedicated to that purpose. All of us were on a mission and while it might have looked chaotic to an outsider, it truly was perfectly orchestrated and planned.

YOU ARE IN THE RIGHT PLACE

As I was finishing up my last few moves to warm-up my coach walked up to me and asked, "How are you feeling, Freddy?" I looked up at him with a grin on my face and replied, "Doing good, coach but I am extremely nervous." I also asked my coach if he saw who was stretching about ten feet away from me. He nodded and said, "Yeah, that is Yuri Chechi from Italy."

My coach might have responded casually but he was a primary source of my nervousness. Yuri was a legend. As one of the top athletes from Italy he competed in seven World Championships and two Olympic Games. This was his seventh time being here. To him this was just like going to the gym to do a few push-ups and getting back home for dinner. Yuri did a relatively simple routine, but it was flawless. Judges could not find a single mistake in his routine. Well they would always find a few small things but it was only visible to the judges and not the public.

To gather myself I began to gaze across the rest of the arena to take my eyes off Yuri and calm my nerves. I gulped as I found a man named Vitally on the other side of the arena. He competed in Belarus in 1992 and won six medals out of a possible seven. Nobody in the world had ever achieved such a feat. My coach also pointed out another gymnast - Alexei Nemov - whom I admired a lot sitting on the tumbling floor stretching just like the rest of us. It was so surreal to think that I was part of the group of athletes I admired for so long.

Somehow, my Dad must have realized by now that I was doubting my abilities to compete against such top athletes. He came over to me after I finished stretching. I began walking to my first event when he said, "Son, look up there." He pointed to the ceiling where all the national flags were hanging. He said, "Do you see that flag?" "Yes, Dad" I replied. He continued his thought by saying, "That flag is up there because of you. You have earned your right to be here. You are in the right place." His simple, iron-clad logic put my mind at ease and allowed my nerves to calm themselves. For that I will forever be appreciative.

Over the next three days we had scheduled training sessions and dinners with the teams and delegates from other countries. I would spend many hours both before and after training with the athletic trainers who were working on my shoulder. I had almost snapped my tendon about a month earlier during a very cold morning training practicing my signature gymnastics skill. I had been training hard on my special strength sequence that no one in the world had ever performed or as a matter of fact seen before. That was a one armed strength move on the rings and extremely stressful on my shoulders. Although tender and painful the tendon was still intact that I could compete, so I needed to take care of my shoulder in between trainings.

Just like in life, groups and cliques began to form and countries began to separate from one another. The old adage "birds of a feather flock together" could not have been more accurate. Some athletes wanted to party while others wanted to be left alone. Some had shown themselves to be very humble while others were quite braggadocios. Don't get me wrong, I am a big believer in ego. When it comes to competition however, my motto has always been to let my actions do the talking. Once I salute and jump onto the apparatus that is when my ego comes through and I let my attitude shine. After I finish and hit the floor, I am no longer competing and therefore I must be as humble as possible.

It was also ego that divided the top athletes in the world into two categories. Some were humble and appreciative of the opportunity they were given while others were much less humble. It showed in the way they treated the people around them including their helpers. I am a true believer that people will not always remember what you have done but will always remember how you made them feel. So, my mission was to not just be great at performing as an athlete but to also connect with everyone around me and be respectful. You must always let your actions leave the impression.

The first night we had a dinner it was made for all the athletes at the camp. By now, I had already befriended not only my personal helper and guide but also a couple of other guides, trainers and helpers from other teams as well. I asked my guide, "So, what is going on with dinner?" He replied, "Well, all of the athletes will be gathered in this arena to have dinner. Helpers will have a break and have to figure out where they can get food but we will be back after you guys are done eating." I was surprised that there would be such a division between athlete and trainer so I asked my guide, "How come you guys can't come in?" He responded, "Well, that is the rule." At this point I knew that the situation wasn't morally right so I asked, "Hey! How about I go with you guys and I will eat whatever you guys are eating?" Their eyes lit up as they were thinking, "Wow! A world-class gymnast is willing to spend time with us and appreciate our efforts and doesn't see himself as superior or inferior." I asked my coach and the team if they were comfortable with my decision. My coach was especially encouraging and told me that I could "absolutely" go. So, with permission to leave we all set out from training camp and into town and had a really great time!

By the next day I had connected with some great athletes and some of my idols and role models. We exchanged techniques and ideas about training as well as different strategies that have helped each one of us over the years. I realized there is something about being at a high level that once you are there, no one questions your ability because you have already made it. There is a special sort of mutual respect amongst everyone who is competing. Everyone knows what you have to go through just to get to the world stage, the amount of pain you have to endure, the perseverance through injuries and the many hours at the gym away from friends, family, holiday gatherings, birthday parties and other events. You have to stay and train when everyone else is having fun. You see this phenomenon frequently. People who are successful have worked hard for their success. Still, they love to share their ideas with others and see others become successful as well.

The night before the competition, after meeting with my coach to decide on final strategies and which skills are going into my routine as well as which skills are coming out, the version for my routine I would be performing the next day was finalized. I felt that I needed to spend some time focused and getting myself centered.

After having trained for three straight days with the people I looked up to as idols and role models, I realized that I belong here. I realized that I earned my spot and at this point, I needed to get my mind focused on competing. I needed to be prepared because once I salute the judges, I must unleash the beast. My motto has always been: "Watch me and enjoy!"

VISUALIZATION PROCESS

I asked Carlos if we could go somewhere that had some peace and quiet and preferably somewhere in nature away from all the noise. We ended up going to a nearby national park and jungle where the only noises you could hear were birds and waterfalls. I spent an hour visualizing and going through my entire routine. I spent an hour mentally preparing, in the core of my body, how I would move and how I would squeeze every single muscle in my body as I went through my routine. I spent that hour visualizing perfection.

It is not enough to just visualize and see yourself doing something; you have to actually feel it. You have to feel it as if you are sitting in a 4D theatre where not only do you see the images playing out in your mind's eye but you are also experiencing the wind, droplets of water, the smells, the warmth of the lights, and everything else which adds realism to an experience. For visualization to be effective you must immerse yourself in all your senses. You must completely experience your vision from all angles. When I visualized I would make sure that I could feel my arms and the weight they were bearing and how my fingers wrapped around the bars, squeezing them when I would swing. I would feel the blood rushing to my toes and then a burst of acceleration, the breeze blowing past my face. When I would perform a skill I would feel the pressure in my hands and feet and when I would dismount and land on the floor I would visualize every cell on the bottom of my feet making contact. I would be able to adjust until the landing was absolutely perfect. Then, I would salute and celebrate!

I would go over this over and over until I would actually feel physical exhaustion from the routine. I would also simulate the moments where I had to take deep breaths. This is very crucial as well because knowing when you are going to breathe is deceptively simple and yet very difficult to do when you are doing a gymnastics routine. You have to time your breathing in between strong bursts of energy releases to be able to battle the inevitable anaerobic depletion of your ATPs during a routine where your muscles are continuously firing without release for over a minute. Sometimes before your dismount you can't feel your hands anymore and have the sensation that you could not possibly hold on any longer. Many times when I teach young athletes at the higher level on the rings, I remind them to breath in a handstand which is one of the hardest handstands in gymnastics, due to the rings and straps being unstable and as a gymnast you must squeeze many muscle groups and exert a lot of force to make it look like you are not moving. When I ask these athletes to breathe when they are in the handstand at first they believe that it's impossible because they have to struggle to just hold the rings still and hold the handstand. I always laugh and say by the time you are ready for a high level rings routine where many strength skills are performed back to back, this will be the only time that you can actually take a breath.

At 6 a.m. my alarm goes off and I wake up suddenly with a rush of anxiety and excitement coursing through my veins. Competition day has arrived! I walk toward the balcony of our high-rise hotel facing the ocean and while admiring the beauty of the view take in a deep breath of crisp, cool fresh air. My ears and heart are soothed by the still silence of the early morning. I spend a few minutes recognizing how hard I have worked, and for so many years I persevered just to be in this moment. I started thinking that by this time tomorrow, it will all be over.

Shortly after this, my coach came over and we went for breakfast. After reviewing one final time what my strategy will be for the day, we head downstairs to the lobby and wait for our bus to take us to the arena. Unlike the last time however, the bus is utterly silent. The many conversations that were strange and orchestral are now so quiet I can focus on the beatings of my own heart. Most athletes were either "in their zone" or in their own mental bubble as they mentally prepared for the day ahead. No one was talking. Everyone was thinking about what they had to do.

Although everyone had their own rituals and their own system to get themselves into the highest peak performance state, it seemed we all agreed that at that time there would be no more conversations. We spent this time in our own heads and in our own hearts.

The bus pulled up and we were walking into the arena through the holding area. Unlike last time, thousands of people filled the stands. It seemed very strange because the first day the arena was calm and empty but now is filled with all the people who paid to come and watch this spectacular gymnastics event. There was such an intense noise with the audience screaming and cheering. This was the real deal.

The training room was next to the arena and the athletes could use it to warm-up and perform routines. Every athlete there was going through their regimen in a studious manner. Each movement and action was carefully calculated and under the watchful eye of their coaches and trainers. Preparation for the event was not trivial.

The Olympic Committee had changed the rules of warming up on the apparatus when audiences are present. We had to warm-up on separate pieces of equipment in another room instead and then march in and compete on different equipment. With a sport like gymnastics, warm-up has a lot to do with feeling of velocity, bounce, the stiffness and softness of equipment and how that will impact your performance. It was really hard to recreate an exact replica of what you were competing on in the preparation room. Regardless of how perfect you have warmed up and trained in the preparation room, when you are competing on the podium, the bar may have a little bit more bounce or be a bit stiffer and you have to adjust. You will only know what the bar is doing when you perform a gymnastics skill and by that point, you do not have the opportunity to readjust. It must be an immediate decision and an immediate adjustment – a reflex. It is a reflex that has been developed through years of practice and performance.

Although we were in the preparation room for only thirty minutes before we marched in, on to the podium, it felt like it had been more than ten hours.

I could not wait to get out into the competitive arena.

Carlos came to me and said, "Hey Freddy, ready to march in? We're lining up by countries and you are going to be in line number five." I looked over to my coach and he nodded his head with approval and said, "You are ready." Without responding I put on my jacket and went to the lineup.

We started marching in and as we got closer and went through the tunnel that I walked through days earlier, I heard the sound of pounding music and the roar of thousands of people who were here to see the event. It all became deafeningly loud and as I drew closer, my heart also became deafeningly loud.

As I walked through the opening to the arena I marched to the designated area where the countries were lining up. I noticed that I had a big smile on my face and was truly happy to be there and amongst the greatest athletes in the world. We were all going to leave our marks on this World Championship event and set a new standard! Unbeknownst to many, every four years the Olympic committee looks at the performances at the World Championships and the Olympics and decides to rewrite the rules. This time the rewrite of the rules would be based on our performances.

After everyone lined up and the officials started their announcements welcoming all the countries, their delegates, and the Olympic Committee officials, my eyes turn skyward. I found the flag and when I saw it I remembered what my Dad had said three days earlier. "That flag is up there because of you." his voice rang in my mind. It was a comforting and stabilizing thought. Although, minutes later the sense of responsibility hit me that I will also be responsible for the results of that flag and our country. It was not just for me any more.

After the national anthems were played, all athletes dispersed to their appropriate events. In men's gymnastics we have six apparatus': Floor Exercise, Pommel Horse, Rings, Vaults, Parallel Bars and High Bar. After we dispersed to our particular apparatus we waited for our turn to show the world why we were here. During the wait it was vital to make sure you kept your body warm and maintain focus.

As mentioned before, the warm-up time was in a preparation room and now we were waiting our turn on the competition floor. Within seconds, you have to get your body revved up to perform at hundred-percent efficiency. This requires an athlete to "turn it on" almost immediately, like flicking a switch that would put you into a state of heightened sensory acuity. This way you are able to make any adjustments that are needed in the apparatus if it is not exactly how you expected it to be. With little warning and even less time I had to shut out everything external and turn it off. This was required so that I could be fully present for what was about to happen!

As I sat and waited for my turn I heard the first few gymnasts completing their routines and how the crowd reacted. They went crazy with excitement! It was at this moment I remembered that if I looked up and started paying attention to everyone else's routine, I could easily lose focus.

Interestingly, there is amazing psychology behind this which I was lucky enough to recognize years earlier. When you are looking at other athletes and you watch them perform amazingly flawless routines you begin to think to yourself, "oh no, that was so good! I absolutely cannot make a mistake now because if I do they will take the Championship." The fact that you are focusing so heavily on not making a mistake can be a mistake in and of itself causing an athlete to make a mistake in their routine.

After all, what you put your focus on will expand and will capture your energy flow.

The other side to this is that if you look at them and they actually mess up their routine, you have an opening. Then you know that if you hit every point of your own routine, you have got them. The problem with that is that you might also take the situation too lightly and because you think you have margin for error, you take it and become too relaxed. You can lose focus because you think you have the Championship in your pocket. This will also cause you to make a mistake. It's a double-edged sword, neither of which is a good edge. If they do well you might lose focus because the task has become too difficult and if they perform poorly you might lose focus because you are overconfident. Both situations lead to mistakes being made.

This would lead me to an interesting dilemma. On one hand I wanted to look up and watch everyone's routine because, after all, this is the World Championships and these are the absolute best athletes in the world. On the other hand, I knew I had to stay focused and kept thinking to myself, "keep to yourself and remain focused. This is not for your entertainment. You are one of them." So I decided to keep my head down and continue visualizing and focusing on what I had to do to perform. The waiting continued and was agonizingly long.

Soon however, it was my turn. I stepped onto the podium and walked up the stairs past the previous gymnast after he had finished his routine. I walked towards the chalk box, readjusted my hand grips and started applying chalk to my hands. The smell of the chalk, its taste and how it slightly stung my eyes were all part of a familiar process I performed each and every time before I competed. I fastened my grips and looked up to see my coach readjusting the mats under the rings on which I would be competing. It took the judges about two to three minutes to come up with the scores for the previous gymnast but it seemed like forever.

THE ZONE

During that time I stood with my feet slightly apart with a very strong stance. My fists were clenched, my chest was up and I was looking towards the sky with my eyes closed. I was getting in "the zone." I was visualizing, yet again, but this time I was visualizing for the last time before my event. In my mind I went through the routine one more time and allowed my muscles to feel the pressure of the rings, the momentum of the swings, the pull of gravity and the contraction of my muscles during all the strength moves and strength holds before finally dismounting.

When I opened my eyes my coach was standing quietly next to me. Through our experience together he knew not to interrupt me and to give me space when I was visualizing. Seeing that I opened my eyes and was focused he gave me a nod and said, "Freddy, this is your event. You have got this, just do what you have always done for the past several months during all those rigorous training sessions. You got this." I nodded my head and noticed that the green light had illuminated. The judges were ready for me.

I walked onto the landing mats and stood right under the rings tower. I kept my eyes down at the floor for a second and refocused myself and got psyched up. With one last deep breath I fully relaxed my mind and body.

I remembered how far I had come. I remembered how many odds I had to beat to get here. I was the same guy that was told he would never make a good gymnast or even be a competitive gymnast. I was the same guy several years later who was now at the World Championships and ready to salute the judges and perform my first event as a world-class competitive gymnast.

I let my confidence swell and take over while a rushing level of calm washed over me. I looked up and saluted the judges. In response, the head judge raised his arm holding a green flag which meant they were ready to look at my routine. I remember the judge giving me a nod as well with a smile, acknowledging my presence.

I acknowledged in return and got ready to jump up to the rings. My coach lifted me up and held me while I adjusted my grip with a strong grasp. As I was hanging still, he gave me a tap on my hips signifying, in a nonverbal manner, good luck. I took one last deep breath into my lungs, as I began my routine.

Instantly, all noise in the arena stopped and all lights were dimmed. It seemed as if I was in a tunnel and I could only see a small area in front of me. This is what happens when your entire focus is pinpointed on one single moment. This occurs when you are fully present in the moment and the world seems like it has stopped moving.

I performed one skill after another; one strength move after another. I felt the familiar feeling and it seemed as if I had done this many times over. I could even hear the voice of my coach saying, "breathe...breathe..." which I heard at certain parts of my routine. The effects of those deep breaths in specific moments allow your muscles to not go into acidosis. In layman's terms, it keeps you from "gassing out" right before dismount.

My routine had full difficulty. It had the same difficulty value as the Italian Olympian Yuri Chechi. I hit the maximum difficulty that I could have had on the rings, which was hard to do at this event. The rings were indeed my best event and I felt confident in my abilities. As I finished my last skill I began focusing and readying myself to do the dismount. I pulled the trigger and did my bail to swing. I dismounted into a double-flip off the rings and landed on my feet. I saluted the judges and as I turned around, my coach was already behind me. As he shook my hand I could see the joy and pride in his face.

I was so deeply focused that it came as a shock when the crowd roared and the cadence became louder and louder as if the volume had suddenly been turned up and the lights had been turned back on. I was returning back to reality and out of "my zone."

A reporter took several interesting pictures of me that day. One of the most interesting ones to me was immediately after I finished my first routine and was shaking my coach's hand. The expression on my face was very strange and I remember thinking to myself "Wow, I spent so many years training to be a world-class gymnast and it all came down to these last sixty seconds. Now, it's all over."

You don't get a chance to redo what you just did and if it was not for all the hard work and the entire process that I systematically went through, I would never have been able to accomplish that goal. An important distinction was that no matter what the outcome and results of the scoring was, I must stay unattached to the results and the score. I knew I had truly done my best and regardless of the actual score, I had reached my desired outcome.

This was only the first event. There were five more events to go and regardless of having the leading score or not, I had to maintain composure and focus throughout the entire competition. There were other events to follow and I had to refocus myself for each and every one. The rings event was over and there was no longer any point in thinking about it. I fixed my focus on what was to come next.

Instead of thinking about the entire competition it is best to take the big championship one event at a time. Once you are done with one event, your sole focus must immediately fall to the next one. Not the event that was just completed or the one after the current one but all focus must be channeled on the present; the NOW.

This experience at the World Championships changed my life. The lessons that came into focus were lessons I have been taking with me throughout my life. Those were also the lessons that helped me make it through medical school and to become a successful entrepreneur.

The most important lesson is that success is definitely a journey. The journey is rarely a straight path and is not about the results. It is about who you have to become to achieve the results you desire. Who I became in order to be at the World Championships will be everlasting.

*"The ultimate end of life is
the development of character."*

- Aristotle

The obstacles that I had to face and the fears I had to overcome, the injuries that I had to heal, the failures and rejection I had to endure, and most importantly the fears and limiting beliefs of those around me are all tools that I acquired and use to face similar challenges in my life. I had to conquer and overcome those fears and limiting beliefs by taking responsibility for my own actions and crushing any and all excuses that would hinder my progress. I had to conquer and fight for my dream, for my *im*possible dream.

Bonus Material
Get clarity on your goals so you can get started towards your outcome today. I will walk you through this process.

Download:
www.LivingImpossibleDreams.com/bonus/clarity

CLARITY

In the zone and ready for the judges to give me the green light.

Freddy B.
1996 WORLD CHAMPIONSHIPS

CHAPTER
3

STEP-1

MINDSET

*"Our decisions and actions are based on
the desire to avoid pain or gain pleasure."*

- Freddy Behin

PLAYING WITH FIRE

As children we learn that if you put your hands in fire you will get burned. The way we associate this thought with our future actions is either through personal experience or observing it happening to someone else. The experience becomes embodied if we actually burn our own hand and understand the associated pain. However, on many occasions we see someone else's pain and assume this could also happen to us.

It is true however that you might be able to place your hand in fire and not be burned. After all, if your hand is moving fast enough and does not stay in the fire long enough, you can avoid being burned. The fire is therefore a metaphor for our true conversation; limitations and limiting beliefs. In this chapter we are going to examine facts and absolutes versus a fact with a low probability of truth and how they are impacted by time. Perhaps it's a one-in-a-million chance that something may not be true, or it may just not be true to you. But however small the chance may be, it still exists.

While yes, fire does burn and I am certainly not suggesting you to go and find out for yourself, the simple idea is that even though a burn from a fire is a limitation there are always ways around it. The moment you accept that fact, your brain will start looking for possibilities and solutions to succeed until the one-in-a-million chance becomes a reality.

Have you ever said to yourself:
"If he can't do it, then certainly I cannot do it?"

YOUR SELF IMAGE

One of the most interesting things that I have noticed as a competitive gymnast is that the ability a person possesses is directly proportional to how they view themselves. There is a definitive correlation between how you view your abilities and what you can achieve. Your level of success is related to your imagination.

In a sport like gymnastics, I have seen athletes place obstacles in their path and be unable to achieve success. Often, this is due to how they imagine themselves and their inability to do so has stopped them from achieving a specific skill or activity. Their physical abilities were not the issue; it was their mental ability and their failure to visualize themselves actually achieving their goal.

I recognized the same issue in medical school while doing surgeries with the limitations of doing the perfect procedure. For example, if I had to make a suture, I would imagine making that perfect suture or the perfect stitch and then I would create it perfectly.

Much of the time, the process was not that difficult. It was simply my beliefs about whether I could accomplish something or not that would impact my ability to do so. It is the mental barriers and our belief that we can accomplish something that gets in the way more often than physical skill or ability.

A famous boxer once said, "you know before you get in the ring if you will be beat or if you will be triumphant." In other words, how a task, challenge, outcome or goal is viewed and how it fits into your skill level or resources makes all the difference. At this point you have created a mindset regarding that task and whether or not it will be possible for you to accomplish. Henry Ford said, "Whether you think you can or whether you think you can't, you're right." Your mindset decided whether you succeed or fail.

This phenomenon of being a prisoner to your own limiting beliefs exists in animals as well. Have you ever wondered how the elephants in circus stay put being tied to a twig?

When the elephant is just a little baby elephant its trained by strapping his leg to a big log. Of course with its little size and weight it has no chance to get himself free, even though it tries relentlessly for days and weeks. Eventually it accepts its fate that with a rope around his foot it will assume that he has no way out. Eventually when the elephant has reached full adult size and even though it posses the strength to rip a tree off the ground, it carries the belief that was instilled in him as a baby elephant and with a small twig and a rope to his leg he will stay put, believing that since he could not get out of it as a baby, that it must be still true, hence being trapped by self imprisonment.

The same limiting belief occurs on fleas. Fleas can reportedly jump about 7 inches high and 13 inches far. That makes the fleas, relative to their body size, the best jumpers in animal kingdom. After placing the fleas in a jar and closing the lid, they will start bouncing and jumping trying to escape. Every time they try to escape they hit the lid and fall back down. Eventually after hundreds of attempts they stop jumping with force and adjust to the height of the jar so they won't hit the lid. Soon they realize that they can not escape and become accustomed to that fact that there is a lid and there are limits. Interesting enough, when the lid is removed they continue to jump only as far as they did with the lid on. They now have accepted this limitation as a fact. They believe that they are never going to escape these confines. They have a valid reason because they hit their head so many times to the lid. They are convinced that it will be their fate from now on. These fleas will never try jumping higher than this limit, as a matter of fact they wont even bother looking up and confirming that the lid is no longer there. They become the prisoner of their own minds. In other words they believe that due to their past experiences and results they will be getting the same results in the future. In other words they believe that their future will equal their past.

Your mindset is the key to finding ways to overcome obstacles and adversity. How you view yourself and your abilities determines whether there is a high wall of excuses and limitations around you and ultimately whether you will achieve the goal or fail before you even try.

Wouldn't it be great if you could take control of your mindset? The way you approach an action and the mindset you have either pushes you forward towards achievement and success or it will devise excuses, barriers and limitations that will sabotage your attempts at achieving what you desire.

"Your reality is shaped by your thoughts.
You become what you think.
Your thoughts govern your actions to keep you
consistent with your identity and
who you think you are."

- Freddy Behin

The reality is that if you approach a task from the outlook that it cannot be accomplished, you will regrettably do whatever is necessary to remain congruent and aligned with your self-limiting thought pattern. There are three questions I asked myself that helped me with my career as a gymnast, a medical doctor and as an entrepreneur. There will be major differences in the outcomes and results that you achieve dependent on how you choose to answer these following questions:

How do you view yourself? – What is your self-perception? Do you believe that you are pre-programmed with certain skill levels or do you believe that there is always a way to succeed regardless of whether the task is unfamiliar or that you have to learn a new skill?

Do you believe that talent plays a major role in achieving your dreams? – Is it talent, or hard work? Can hard work, practice and dedication have the same results for someone as a talented person? Besides your self-concept and how you view your skills, it's also important to know how you view your successes.

Do you believe you are destined to succeed? – Is the choice to succeed or fail within your control or is your belief that no matter what you do you will always fail? In other words is success externally affected beyond your control? Or do you believe that based on the talent and abilities you are given you have a limitation, leaving you with a fixed mindset versus a growth mindset where you can learn and improve the skill set instead.

Your mindset is literally the most vital tool you have and with the proper mindset, nothing is *im*possible.

> *"Talent is cheaper than table salt.*
> *What separates the talented individual*
> *from the successful one is a lot of hard work."*

- Stephen King

MY PATH OF BEING A GYMNAST

When I was twelve years old I had a dream that I would one day become a competitive gymnast. I always loved watching gymnastics and I thought to myself, "How cool is it to be able to do all those flips?!" It was amazing to me and when I tried to do them myself it seemed extremely difficult. I soon learned that you must have a real expert teaching you and not to rely on an average gym coach for such a specialized skill. I learned this lesson through the costly price of breaking my foot.

When I approached my gym coach and asked him, "How can I do a twist in my flip?" he replied with, "Just turn faster." I did exactly as instructed and performed a flip while turning as fast as I could.

I wound up landing off the gymnastics mat and ended up breaking my foot.

The important lesson to be learned is that there is a process and flow to everything and this process must be respected, not rushed. I also learned that it is important to identify who you should and should not listen too. Regardless of this minor setback and having a cast on my leg for weeks, I learned how to do a handstand on my crutches. Since I could not tumble, but my arms still functioned perfectly, I decided to concentrate on learning those skills. I enjoyed the process and enjoyed learning so I decided that I wanted to become more serious in my pursuit as a competitive gymnast.

My dreams almost ended as quickly as they began however, when I was told by the people that I respected and trusted the most that I had no chance of becoming a competitive gymnast. If I would have listened to them though, I would have never achieved what I have achieved in life. Instead, I decided that I was going to show up for every practice and every training session as well as keep a journal to track my progress.

Of course, all the good gymnasts were getting the attention and the coach was only spending time with them so I had to figure out how to coach myself. Every day I would watch and observe the best gymnasts there and I would look at what they did and how they did it. I would study their workout habits. Instead of looking at what was impossible, I would observe how other gymnasts were making it possible.

Ultimately, the important question was if any of the athletes I watched each and every day had any skills that were different from me. Were they more talented, or more muscular? Were they more flexible than I was? If the answer was yes to any of these questions then that simply meant I was lacking resources, not ability. Nothing more, nothing less.

Throughout the years I have always been asked about gymnastics and people would say, "Wow, I am not that flexible!", "I am not that strong!" or, "No way, I would die if I were to attempt that." People assume that I was a naturally-born gymnast when in reality it is their thought patterns and their mindset that kept them limited and not achieving what they desired. If you look at the best Olympians, they all started out as being less talented and less capable versions of themselves. They all started off with weaknesses. In essence, they all started by "not being that flexible" or "not being that strong".

The notion of thinking that you have to be good at something before you start doing it is what prevents people from having a winning result and a successful mentality. The fact is that anyone that has ever achieved anything in life had to start at the beginning and work their way up. This preconceived notion is fueled by the fact that we only get to see the glory of winners and champions and rarely see the hard work that goes on behind the scenes. No one notices you when you are doing all the hard work, but they notice you when you get the results. So, think of your mindset as the key to unlocking the power and talent that you already possess and it starts with seeing the possibilities around you. When I saw the possibility of being a competitive gymnast was one-in-a-million, I took it. I went out and I found that one chance.

As you may see on television, many athletes have a ritual before they begin. My personal rituals while competing included clearing my mind prior to competition and visualizing my movements. I wanted to make sure that I was focused on what I actually wanted to achieve.

On the day of the competition I would walk into the arena and I would visit all the apparatuses. Prior to going into the locker room, I would get acquainted with the environment around me. I would assess the bars, the rings and the tumbling floor and would test them to see if they were springy or stiff and would make a decision on how to approach each one.

Next, I would imagine or visualize myself succeeding on the podiums. Once I was dressed to compete and prepared to do warm-ups, minutes before being ready to salute, I would imagine being up on the podium and saluting the judges triumphantly after hitting each skill and technique within my routine flawlessly.

Don't get me wrong, I am not going all woo woo on you. I am not suggesting and expect you to think this is some spiritual awakening or that there is some magic involved. It is a simple concept that ultimately if you can not imagine the end result in your mind there is a smaller chance that you will actually be able to create the end result. You can only create what you can imagine and perceive in your mind. So you must be able to imagine it and see it in your mind first. Same as an artist must have a clear image in their mind before the creation of their master piece.

My visualization had three components:

1. First, I would see myself doing the routine from a distance, like an outsider looking in on what was going on. I would see my routine exactly the same way a judge would see it. I would visualize it exactly the way the audience would see it as well and ensure that the picture in my mind was congruent with the specific result that I wanted to achieve. This was very crucial for me. How I saw myself in my mind was going to be exactly what I would achieve. I would envision myself performing a skill and then I would see them again performed perfectly. Lastly, I followed my visualization all the way through the end as I would absolutely nail my dismount and landing and then salute victoriously to the waiting judges.

2. Second, my visualization turns inward. I visualize my entire routine a second time but the perspective is my own. I would see everything I was doing from my own viewpoint and envision myself doing it perfectly.

3. Lastly, the third step was the most crucial part. I would

engage my senses in the visualization. I would see, feel, and hear myself doing my routines. I would stand and move my body in ways similar to what my mind's eye was seeing. I would feel every muscle fiber that needed to squeeze, twitch or stretch as I went through the various techniques. The air on my face as I was flipping with velocity would feel cool and fast. My hands, slipping around the apparatus and every other aspect of my routine would be visualized as if I was actually performing it. I call this step the "4D Visualization."

The three-step visualization process would put me in the right mindset so that when I raised my hand and saluted the judge, I already knew what the outcome would be. Not only that, I had already done the routine, three separate times, perfectly in my mind. Many people do not realize that when a gymnast finally gets to perform their routine at a competition they have been waiting for quite some time. There is a time delay between when they warm-up and get a turn to perform. Their bodies may have cooled down, their concentration may have broken or they fail to recognize that the equipment may not be the same as what they had warmed-up on. The reality is that what is seen on TV is that perfect execution. That is because the gymnast is able to adjust and place themselves in the right mindset knowing they only get one chance to perform and it is all over in a matter of seconds.

Sometimes in life we only get one shot at doing something extraordinary and it is paramount that we have the right mindset when those opportunities knock. Having rehearsed in your mind and felt in your soul the steps and actions needed for success will allow you to achieve your best and overcome any obstacle.

The takeaway from this chapter is that you must envision yourself on the podium of your journey. You must see and feel yourself achieving perfection to create the perfect outcome.

> *"You are not bound by the same beliefs*
> *of someone saying it is not possible.*
> *Do not give into that thought.*
> *No matter what."*

- Freddy Behin

Even if you have witnessed someone else not achieve their goals, it should not in any way make you doubt your own abilities.

Success does not happen by accident. Success is earned through hard work and a dynamic way of life.

There is a pattern to the lives of successful people. The single-most important aspect is that they always see themselves succeeding. That does not mean that they never fail. Successful people fail the same way as unsuccessful people. The difference is that successful people make adjustments and "get back on the bar", just like a gymnast. They focus themselves, get chalked up, and jump right back up again.

> *"Progress without change is impossible."*

- Freddy Behin

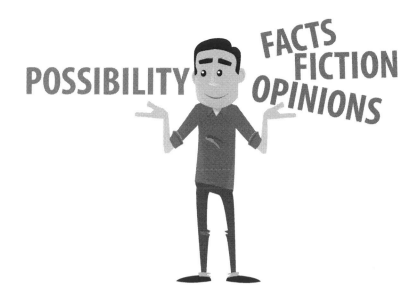

BEWARE OF 'FACTS' AND 'STATS'

I clearly remember being a freshman at UCLA and identifying specific differences between each group of students. Each academic department was unique and surrounded me with a variety of students ranging from the wealthy to the not wealthy and the struggling college students in between. Some students drove their Mercedes-Benz or BMW to class while others walked or took the bus. Also differing amongst the various demographics of students was their desire to succeed and I found that to be very surprising.

Although the level of desire for success varied between the groups of students, the level of anxiety and teamwork was very distinct amongst the academic departments. Students from more competitive departments focused around Medical or Pre-Med degrees such as biology, chemistry, physiology or neuroscience were much more anxious about their performance, exhibited a larger fear of sharing knowledge or cooperating with one another, and were enjoying college less on average than students from other departments. Students from other departments seemed to network with one another much more frequently and productively and exhibited a higher sense of enjoyment throughout the process.

During my first year at UCLA I studied computer science and was very interesting in software development and the creation of new ideas that were able to "come alive" on a computer. I was quickly noticed by my teachers as being a sharp software developer and was able to accelerate through my computer science classes. I was offered an opportunity to work on highly complex software development projects at the Cardiovascular Research and Electrophysiology Department. This software was to assist in understanding electrical chaos in cardiac fibrillation and reentering spiral waves in diseased hearts. In simpler terms, the end result would prevent patients with cardiac disease and pacemakers from dying due to chaos or irregular electrical patterns in their hearts, an Artificial Intelligence Pacemaker.

This project allowed me to associate with some of the best medical doctors and cardiac researchers in the world. I quickly became fascinated with the world of medicine and more specifically, cardiology. Based on the recommendations and encouragement from one of the doctors I wanted to work with I decided to switch my major to physiological sciences.

As excited as I was to start this new chapter in my life and begin building a new future for myself I quickly realized that the level of competition in these medical classes was extremely high. Somehow, the concept of teamwork in medical academia did not exist. Students did not want to share notes with one another or help one another understand concepts due to the fear they had about being cut from the program. Every student wanted to take advantage of every edge that they had to ensure they tested on the right side of the bell curve during exams.

Naturally, this was very discouraging and pre medical studies became a very lonely path to travel. Towards my third year the realization struck me that if I was to gain a spot in medical school some miracles were going to have to happen. Not only did I need a perfect GPA but I also needed a perfect MCAT (Medical College Admission Test) score. Additionally, pre-med students also needed to have completed significant research and have networking connections and references from practicing doctors. Of course, it also would have helped to have physicians for parents as well. Almost all the odds were stacked against me as well as the constant reminder of others around me who were failing. Even people who matched almost all of the criteria to be accepted into medical school were not getting in and still had to wait several years for an interview.

Interestingly, when people who are more qualified than you fail based on the same criteria it becomes very easy to assume that you will also fail. Statistically, you probably have an even less chance than they did at achieving a positive outcome. Even though logic dictates that the thought pattern makes sense, the key learning factor here is not to give in to the statistics but to find a way to defy them. It becomes even more imperative that you find an exception to the rule.

All you have to ask of yourself is the following: "Is it really true that all of the above criteria must be met to be accepted into medical school? Has there ever been a single student who was accepted into medical school with a mediocre MCAT score and a mediocre GPA? If so, what would set me apart from the rest of my peers so that my GPA and MCAT scores will not be priority?" The moment you create a tear in the fabric of minimal requirements in your own mind is the moment that you have opened a window of opportunity. Suddenly, there is a chance that exists for you to achieve your dreams. It may be a one-in-a-million chance, but it is possible. And if it is possible then you must entertain the idea that you will be that very exception and will find success.

*"You can not change anything
unless your mind changes it first."*

- Freddy Behin

GENETIC ADVANTAGE
WHAT IS THE TRUTH?

Are all NBA players tall and all gymnasts short? Do you have to be tall to be a great basketball player or short to be a great gymnast? If you answered "No", then you have been paying attention. Although it makes life much easier to be tall when playing basketball or short when practicing gymnastics, there is no correlation between height and success.

On the matter of height, I would like to address a very common question. Consistently I am asked about gymnastics and if that will make someone short or if practicing basketball will help make someone tall. Unfortunately, the answer to these questions is a very strong "NO." It does not matter how many thousands of hours someone can practice basketball, you will never exceed the genetics of height given to you by your ancestry. There is always a margin for error but this margin consists of a few inches. Five foot tall parents rarely produce children who cross the six foot mark. The same is true for taller parents. Rarely do tall parents produce a child who is short. The only times this correlation is inaccurate is when there are metabolic disorders and deficiencies or hormonal imbalances that alter height.

A perfect example is my friend, Tony Robbins. He is 6'7" tall because of a pituitary tumor which produced an excess of growth hormone and caused his bones to grow at a much larger rate. I can assure you that Tony does not play basketball every day nor has he ever been considered to be an exceptional basketball player. Besides the nutritional factors that can hinder growth, injuries and heavy pressure to the growth plates of a child can also hinder growth.

In conclusion, no; you will not be short if you do gymnastics. Also, the pressure placed on the body by gymnastics is not enough to close growth plates. The fact is that when you see these athletes on TV, you notice the shorter gymnasts are the better gymnasts because they have greater leverage and center of gravity. They also work very hard at their training. Taller gymnasts must work harder but that does not mean that shorter gymnasts did not have to work!

This keeps with the concepts I have been teaching you throughout this book. All you need to do is look for possibilities. Has there ever been an exceptionally short NBA player? There are many but one of my favorites is the giant Muggsy Bogues. At 5'3", he was one of the shortest players in the history of the NBA. He played for the Bullets, Hornets, Warriors and Raptors from 1987 through 2001. He was one of the fastest players in the game and was so exceptional at stealing the ball that he could snatch it from just about anyone!

The lesson here is that if there is a chance for success you must embrace that window of opportunity as well as be willing to put in the work necessary to make that opportunity a reality. The work necessary to succeed is still there and must still be executed to succeed. The fact of the matter is that with people like Muggsy

Bogues, whether he wanted to be a gymnast or a basketball player, he would have been successful. He would find his opportunity, approach it with the right mindset, and do all the work that was necessary to succeed.

ON TO MEDICAL SCHOOL

As I approached the last year of my undergraduate studies at UCLA the reality of the next phase of my growth started kicking in. The excitement of being accepted to medical school as well as the anxiety of not getting accepted into a medical school became more of a reality. I needed to get my medical school application ready and come up with options to make this dream of becoming a doctor also a reality. Many of my peers were hustling to figure out the next step as well.

While connecting with several people who had gone through the process of becoming a doctor as well as some currently enrolled medical students, I discovered a pattern. Almost all students who applied to medical school had the same characteristics in common. If all I had was what the rest of the applicants had I would just blend in. I knew right away that using the same patterns would give me little to no advantage over others. The common characteristics were a high GPA, a high MCAT score, extensive volunteer work in medical field, and also research credits, which applicants put on their personal statements. The biggest common criteria was a story on how medicine has always been the center of their focus and/or an incident in their life where the life of a loved one was threatened inspired them and gave them the drive for wanting to be a doctor.

At this stage of my life I was already an entrepreneur and had formed two businesses. I was operating a software development business as well as gymnastics facility with several hundred students and about 10 employees at the time. I knew that I had different strengths that needed to be shown to the medical school acceptance committee. The fact of the matter is that a perfect GPA and a perfect MCAT score is only relevant in showing that you are able to take tests and have a basic understanding for the basic sciences. It doesn't necessarily mean you will succeed in this field or even have the ability to take your knowledge and apply it further. Unfortunately that is how the most systems choses to pick their applicants since there is not much else setting the applicants apart. I needed to get the committee interested in my application. My personal statement needed to paint a winning picture within the allotted one page. I was wondering how I could avoid saying the same as the other thousands of applicants with an amazing GPA and MCAT scores. Instead I wanted to make the reader want to know more about me so I get invited for an interview

As a young business owner I knew the value of a great team for my operations. I knew that regardless of the background, the key in hiring someone was to see how their strengths will enhance the business and how they will fit the culture and enhance the environment they will be placed in. I believe that being accepted to medical school is practically a job application. Ultimately you are representing your school and your success and failure will be under that schools name. This is why I decided to approach this process as a win-win strategy for both the school and myself. How can I bring value to this school and how will they benefit from having chosen me over another applicant?

The fact of the matter is that success leaves clues and how you have performed in the past dictates pretty closely to how you will perform in the future. Not because of the talents or luck of the draw but because of a formula for success and formula for discipline you have adopted and used to consistently produce the successful results. My job was to paint this picture of success for them and how my approach to what I have accomplished so far would in fact be mirrored in the medical field as well. I chose to elaborate on my strengths and how it would contribute to my success in medicine.

A few of the characteristics that would set me apart included, how my competitive nature and perseverance as a world class athlete could contribute to overcoming challenges in medical school and medical field. As a software developer my analytical mind and approach would allow me to problem solve and see patterns. As a business owner and entrepreneur I have a higher level of understanding on management, finances, responsibility and developing a team, which would allow me to act as a leader in the medical field. Ultimately my love for having a positive impact on peoples lives as a gymnastics coach would translate into a compassionate approach with patience in the medical field. As you can see, I chose to put the focus on what is great about me rather than what I am average at and let the reader see outside of the box why I would be a great choice to receive a spot as a medical student. This strategy allowed me to get an interview and get accepted into medical school.

What I would like to emphasize here for you is that you must think outside of the box when things seem very hard in a competitive arena. Choose to be different in a great way. You have characteristics, experiences and strengths that are unique to you. This combination is what makes you who you are, embrace them and strengthen them further. I have helped several people using this approach to get into medical schools and land higher positions in their fields of choice. When all else is the same, what is that one thing that will set you apart from the rest and what is the one difference that would make the difference?

"Embrace and nourish the one difference that sets you apart from the rest to get a competitive edge."

- Freddy Behin

During my first semester as a medical student I remember that I was really inspired by plastic surgery. My anatomy professor, Dr. Ponce, was a great plastic surgeon and I remember thinking to myself "oh my gosh! How in the world am I going to memorize all of these anatomical features and all of these nerves, veins, arteries, attachments and structures." It was not the fact that I had difficulty memorizing the information; it was that I simply did not have sufficient time to dedicate to the task. I felt like I was falling behind fifty pages every day. This was, when I decided I was not going to succeed studying the traditional way. I needed to find another way. For some reason, my brain was not wired like other medical students and this did not come naturally to me.

After reading every chapter and every section about the anatomy, I started making my own anatomy atlas. I started drawing all of the anatomical parts. Most importantly, I started drawing them from several different perspectives and was able to utilize that instead of only reading the text book. I would spend time drawing nerves, attachments, tendons, muscles, simply everything and color them in. In this way I was able to learn what each anatomical part was in relation to each other. Most importantly, I convinced myself that I was enjoying the process and that studying was not a chore.

I would draw on a whiteboard in my apartment continuously to not only memorize the anatomy but to also embody the structures into my memory. It was this creative method of studying that allowed me to understand the human anatomy so well. I was able to visualize after drawing and could see each physiological part from all angles. This allowed me to solve tough questions and complete difficult projects because I understood the relationships between parts. In essence, I saw a difficult task and tackled it from a new angle. I was able to capitalize on my strengths as a visualizer and diagram the human anatomy for me to be able to recall when needed.

*"You become who you hang out with.
Therefore, proximity to the right individuals is powerful."*

- Freddy Behin

One day I was studying with one of the third-year medical students who had become one of my mentors during college. He was married with a child and was relentless in how he studied. He wanted to become a neurosurgeon which is a pretty difficult field of medicine. The day that we were studying together I confessed to him that I was really fascinated with plastic and reconstructive surgery procedures and that when I become a surgeon I wanted to be able to do so many things. Shortly after I had vocalized that thought I learned a very valuable lesson. He asked me, "Why do you have to wait until you are a plastic surgeon? You need to become one today."

Of course I did not understand what he meant that day. I thought to myself, "How can I become a plastic surgeon in my first semester of med school? I don't even know anatomy very well and I have only been inside an operation room once to which I nearly fainted! Isn't graduation and board exams and residency all required? So, what exactly is he talking about? How in the world am I going to be a plastic surgeon today? I still have many years to go."

Thankfully breaking my thought chain, he explained to me that if you want to be something in life, you have to imagine it and start living it. In other words, do what plastic surgeons do and start today. Start by building the same daily habits they use by setting your mindset into a successful mode.

Also, take actions as habitual rituals that successful surgeons embark upon. I had to get my mindset to believe that I was already a plastic surgeon.

So, I started looking at my mentor, Dr. Ponce, who was a plastic surgeon and my anatomy professor. I had already created an elaborate Atlas of Anatomy which several students wanted to use and made copies of my drawings for their studies. Eventually my anatomy professor found out that I was the artists behind the drawings. Soon my nickname became "Freddy Netter" after the famous anatomy illustrator, Frank Netter. Dr. Ponce was very impressed with my anatomy illustration skills and that helped me build some rapport with him and get closer to learn more about medicine, being a doctor and plastic surgery.

I connected with him and used the opportunity and offered to recreate his lecture notes to include nice diagrams and graphics. This also meant that I was able to spend even more time with Dr. Ponce so that I could learn and study what it really meant to be a plastic surgeon. I was able to learn his habits and mannerisms. After all, the goal was to start living the life of a plastic surgeon.

What I learned was invaluable. Dr. Ponce indulged in certain daily rituals that became habitual in nature. He always woke up very early in the morning and he always dressed in a suit. He also was a gentle man who adhered to a healthy diet and exercise regimen. Dr. Ponce also tackled every task in his life very seriously and was meticulous about the outcome. He also made it a point to help people he met and was a very generous man. When entering a room, Dr. Ponce displayed an extremely confident presence, as if there was nothing that could happen that he could not handle.

Over a period of several years, Dr. Ponce became one of my favorite mentors and friends and I was privileged to spend many hours in the OR (Operating Room) with him. By the time I was in my third year of medical school, I had already performed hundreds of procedures in an OR. I had developed the confidence and the skill set I needed as well as the belief that I actually could be an excellent plastic surgeon as a third-year student.

On weekends when my classmates would go out to clubs or bars I would spend my time learning about new procedures from Dr. Ponce and strengthening my skill sets. I had developed my mindset so that I had a different view of myself, my abilities and of my successes.

My best memories of my time in medical school were when Dr. Ponce would call me at 2 a.m. to invite me to assist him in an emergency or trauma surgery. He knew I would be awake and working on my skills as opposed to other medical students who were sleeping and not doing the extra work necessary to succeed. I knew that this would set me apart from my peers.

> *"To have what others don't have
> you must do what others will not do."*
>
> - Freddy Behin

This is the same gift you must give to yourself. Your mindset is influenced by who you hang out with. If you are around negative people you will adopt a negative mentality. If you are around those lacking success then you will adopt a "lacking" mentality and it will apply to your personal finances, health, relationships and your career.

You must develop the ability to see things better than they are. To create the ability to envision yourself succeeding is vital. You must be able to see yourself at the finish line and understand that the people who hang out with you will dictate how well you accomplish your goals.

Successful people have high standards. If you are around successful people then you will naturally adopt the same set of high standards. This by itself will change your mindset and how you view yourself. With a mindset free from constraining thoughts and excuses, the possibilities are limitless. Simply stated, set high standards for yourself where no excuses will be tolerated.

> *"Strengthen your mind around possibilities"*
>
> - Freddy Behin

Find ways and reasons why success regarding your ultimate outcome or goal is already accomplished. Instead of thinking about all the reasons why you would not succeed and all of the ways you could fail, think about all of the ways you could succeed. When you change your mind you will change your life.

FIXED VS. GROWTH MINDSET

One of my favorite authors is Carol Dweck, a Stanford University psychologist and the author of "*Mindset*." She introduced a simple idea pertaining to two types of mindsets, a Fixed mindset versus a Growth mindset.

Individuals with a Fixed mindset believe in their basic qualities such as their intelligence or talents. Their intelligence and talent is acquired instead of developed. They also believe that talent alone can create success.

People with a Growth mindset however, believe that their abilities can be developed through dedication and hard work. This view creates a love of learning and a resilience that is essential for great accomplishment.

Although during my young adulthood I had not read her book yet I had a hard time accepting that some people had something that would give them an advantage over me. I truly believed that I was capable of whatever it took to achieve anything I wanted while maintaining the realization that I could possibly be missing some resources. I had two options, I either accepted my lack of resources as an excuse and give up on achieving my dream or open my mind to the possibility of success and examine plans B, C, D, etc. until I find what I need to be successful.

If we do not look at the one-in-a-million chance and the possibility that the "impossible" is possible for us, we will never enable our brains to think about the true possibilities in life and be able to act on them.

Bonus Material
Discover your mindset and limiting beliefs.

Download:
www.LivingImpossibleDreams.com/bonus/mindset

MINDSET

CHAPTER
4

STEP-2

DESIRE

"You can move beyond PAIN and FAILURE with DESIRE. DESIRE is like FUEL that propels you no matter what."

- Freddy Behin

PAIN VS. PLEASURE

Early childhood experiences move us towards the idea that life is about finding pleasure and avoiding pain. The more we experience pain in our lives the more our threshold for pleasure decreases. This slowly creates a sense of caution where we live our lives with the intent of avoiding pain at all costs.

When we reach our adult lives we often cease to take action. We simply want to avoid having any pain in life, real or imagined so we often do nothing that would result in pain. Often that stops us from experiencing pleasure. In most cases we get paralyzed due to fear of pain and failure. Adults develop the concept that it is better to not bother trying because trying can lead to failure, which is a form of pain. We often feel it is better to not try and risk getting hurt in the process or possibly getting our hearts broken. Frequently, a broken heart is related to pain.

Therefore, adults begin creating rules around certain behaviors based on the success and failure of others we observe around us. When adults see others in pain we tend to associate that action with negativity and experience it as our own pain.

Having desire is literally like having fuel that provides you with the energy to move forward with commitments that you are trying to accomplish. Desire is correlated with strong reasons for achieving what you want to achieve. It is the "why" behind what you want to do. Everything we do in our lives has a reason behind it. The stronger your "why", the more likely you will stay committed to your outcome.

THE REASON "WHY"

When your "why" is strong enough, desire increases. Coincidentally, when your "why" is scary enough, your desire also increased. Both fear and excitement for pleasure create a desire to achieve. On one hand the desire to achieve is driven by wanting to feel good while on the other, the desire is propelled by the compulsion to avoid pain. When your "why" is strong enough, it will push you towards your goals where you have no choice but to achieve. Simply stated, your "why" provides you with the reason to achieve.

You may ask yourself, "Is desire something that can actually be developed? What if I don't want to do something?" In these instances, your "why" is weak and this chapter will help you cultivate it and make it stronger.

Your "why" fuels your desire and it is related to whether you will experience pain or pleasure if your desire is fulfilled. How often have you said to yourself, "I'm not good at this and I don't like to do it?" Peeling the layers back on this mentality we often find that what causes someone to not enjoy doing something is a lack of pleasurable experiences associated with the action. Simply, we don't like it because we have not experienced success.

Conversely, when we feel that we are enjoying life it is because we feel successful from achieving what we are doing. Ironically, when success is achieved, more success is created. This is because the act of succeeding can be fuel for more success. When you experience success you develop proof that future success is also possible. Because of this it should be no surprise to anyone that when we do not enjoy the tasks and actions we do, we are more likely to also lack success, due to the proof of continued failures in that area. We rarely hear someone in great physical shape who works out daily say, "I hate working out." On the other hand, someone who is not in good physical shape is very likely to say, "I don't like working out."

One of the greatest challenges in our society today is that everyone is looking for instant gratification. We try something once and if immediate results are not achieved it is considered too difficult and we quickly lose interest. Life today is very fast-paced with wireless mobile devices that deliver information at amazing speeds. We have been trained in the last decade to expect things delivered immediately. We get movies on-demand through a small, portable device we carry in our pockets and have more information available to us than the President of the United States twenty years ago.

The challenge is that we have lost the ability to be patient. One of the most common dream-crushers is that we are no longer willing to focus on things that require that little bit of extra time, effort, or attention. Even though we are seeking gratification, if it is not instant gratification then we quickly lose interest.

The end result is not the main thing that stays with us once we have achieved our goal. It is who we become as a result of achieving our goal that has a lasting effect on us. That goal allows us the opportunities to have repeated successes, long after the goal was achieved in the first place. When you look at children playing a video game at an incredible speed and zoom through levels, it is because they have experienced that level of the game before and know what the challenges are at specific points of the game and anticipate the moments. Therefore, the process and the challenge that comes with achieving the goal and how those challenges are handled is what drives you towards success.

It is the journey, not the destination that builds us into the people that we are. If the biggest gift we receive from accomplishing our goal is who we have become during our journey for success, then who we are and what we become is related to the journey. This is based on our decisions and how we have made choices in our lives when obstacles become present as well as when doubt, fear and failure get in our way.

How have you solved the problem? How have you emotionally dealt with each opportunity? I call them opportunities because they are to be used as points of reference. Similar to the moments in a video game when you know that the monster comes out at a specific junction of the game. These points will make your journey to success easier from that moment onward. How we deal with the journey is vital in becoming the person that will achieve the results you desire. Therefore, we must be very motivated by the journey alone.

If we are looking for instant gratification then we are robbing ourselves of the journey. Even if we achieve our goals we are missing a significant component which allows us to achieve repeated future successes and goals. There is a simple formula that I would like to share which I have repeatedly used in every area of my life and it's very easy to do.

As previously mentioned, it is our desire that pushes us forward into achieving impossible dreams. In order to have that desire we must have excitement about what we are doing and the process associated. This means that we have to feel good about the excitement and allow that positivity to enhance all elements of the journey. This includes all of the up's and down's and bumps in the road. Despite these trials and tribulations, we must feel good about the journey because it is the journey that leads us to success. To accomplish this we must maintain our focus on the end results taking one small step at a time while acknowledging our gratitude for every bit of progress that we make.

"Success demands that you focus on your purpose, and move towards your purpose with a decision."

- Freddy Behin

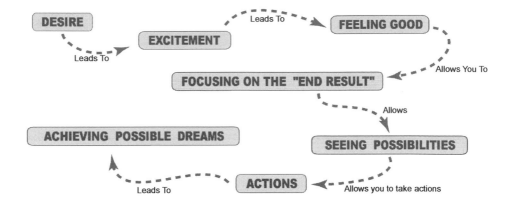

THE MAGIC FORMULA

The above digram depicts the magic formula to success and the self fulfilling cycle that will produce the results. The secret to this formula is in how each step fuels the next. Desire leads to excitement. Excitement leads to feeling good about what you are doing. Feeling good about what you are doing will allow you to focus on the end results and the possibility of success instead of all the difficulties and obstacles. That will lead you to take actions towards your goal. The secret is really in when you can imagine and see the possibility and identify with the end results you will produce. With this identity in your mind, your brain will fight to deliver at all costs, just to stay congruent with your self image. Once you have that, it equals achieving your impossible dreams.

And that's it. We're done with the book. Roll credits! Thank you for reading this far because that was the secret.

But wait! There is more. Let me tell you this little story first.

In my early twenties I noticed a strange phenomenon as a gymnast. It was obvious that most gymnasts had an event apparatus that they were exceptionally proficient in, as well as one or two apparatuses that they struggled on and had a hard time to perform on. The interesting part is that if we time the practice and take records of time spent on every apparatus, we would realize that most of the practice time and focus was spent on the apparatuses that the gymnast was already very good at. In other words less time was actually spent working on improving on the apparatuses at which they struggled at. As subtle as these findings were, the difference in performance was indisputable. The reason was that they were excited for the events that they were proficient at.

When I think back to myself and one of my teammates, Mark, I realize that both of us were opposites. We were completely opposite from one another in each and every way. I was very strong on the rings while Mark was incredible on the pommel horse. He would spend the same amount of time practicing on the pommel horse as I did practicing the rings and in contrast we both spent very little time practicing the events that we were not good at. In csscncc, we were excited for the events that we did well in but found it to be a chore or hard work to practice the other events. Believe me it was a chore and hard work. Regardless, it was mandatory that we practice the other events.

It dawned on me at that moment that, "what if I spent the same amount of time on an event I'm not good at? What if I actually spend more time on that event?" This thought was quickly met with an inner dialogue that replied, "Oh no, the Pummel Horse! How can I spend more time on the Pommel Horse!? My shins would smack against the wooden handles and I would be bruised and hurt very quickly. There is only so much beating a man can take during a workout so why would I want to do that to myself?"

The funny thing is, I did exactly that on the rings. I took all the beating that the rings could dish out but I was enjoying it! It was a fun and an acceptable challenge for me, instead of a chore. This led me to understand that it was not about getting beaten or bruised during practice that mattered to me. The entire reason why

I did not enjoy the aptly named Pommel Horse was because I did not have the right mindset. It had nothing to do with me wanting to or not wanting to do something, it had to do with desire. It was the desire to perform and to shine on the rings rather than get bludgeoned on the pommel horse and just get by. It also had nothing to do with my ability level. It was purely about the time spent on the apparatus I was not very excited to spend time with.

Let us review this paradoxical pattern; pain versus pleasure. Great results and successes bring about feelings of pleasure. The more pleasure a person receives, the more desire they have to take action. Also, more action produces better results. The cycle continues when more pleasure is derived from more results and is very similar to what I experiences on the rings apparatus.

On the other hand, when you experience pain, you receive little to no positive results, your desire lowers. A lack of positive results creates a lack of desire. When desire is lacking there is less want for action. Less action equals poor results and this becomes a vicious cycle.

Understand that all results are dependent on taking action. The only thing that can improve results is changing your desire and taking more action. Taking more action will lead to positive results. This answers the question of why we are very proficient at some things and not very good at others. It also is no surprise why we like to do things that we are good at and avoid the things that are not giving us the positive results. This is why we sometimes say "We aren't good at that" or "I do not like to do that." It's because the negative results leads to less desire.

Things get exciting however, when you decide to change your mind. What if you actually got excited about the process? Imagine the kind of job that you would do or the kind of opportunities that you would have. What would become of your daily habits and what new habits would you adopt that would change your life?

I strongly believe that the majority of people live their lives performing way under their maximum capabilities. People often quit before they have truly tried. Defeat is accepted early in the process to avoid experiencing any displeasure.

Have you ever done anything extraordinary or something that truly seemed impossible? Have you accomplished a feat so great that regardless of any obstacle you knew it had to be achieved because failure was not an option? The reason is because you had a compelling reason "why" behind your actions, driving you and pushing you to accomplishing it. That compelling "why" is the desire to achieve that fuels us to achieve impossible dreams.

I clearly remember at 17 years old that I had qualified to compete at the national championships. I had trained hard that entire year and was very excited. I really wanted to take home a medal, stand on the podium, and in my heart I knew this was achievable. The competition was going really well and I was performing all my routines flawlessly. When I got to the parallel bars, which was my 5th event, I chalked up and prepared for that routine. My coach gave me some last minute instructions and then I saluted the judges signaling that I was ready to perform.

The initial part of my routine was very difficult. There were several skills that needed to be performed consecutively, three of which were blind skills, one after another. Blind skills are skills that are performed without being able to see where your hands need to go on the parallel bars. I would be required to grip the bar without being able to see what I was doing, relying purely on my instincts, timing, preparation, and "gut" feeling. Of course, there was always a chance that I would miss the bar but it was also due to the high-risk nature of this sequence in my routine that it was valued so highly.

I took a deep breath and used my last few seconds before my routine started to focus and get into my mental state. I started my routine and worked my way to the tricky part. I perfectly executed the first and second skill and was preparing to do my third blind skill when I felt my hand shift on the bar. I landed on my middle finger which resulted in a broken and displaced finger. I only had four more skills to perform and the dismount to finish the event. As many gymnasts have the ability to work through their pain, somehow, I put it all together and finished the event.

When I looked at my finger it was clear that it was displaced because it was pointing in the wrong direction. My coach immediately got ice and the trainers came to take a look. After several minutes of observing my finger the consensus from the trainers as well as my coach was that I should stop competing. I immediately thought to myself that "I have come this far and trained for a whole year to be in the national championships. I am so close and only have one event left to go." The problem was that the last event was the high bar event. I needed to use of all my fingers. This situation was compounded when I also realized that the finger that was broken was also the hand used for many one-armed skills. Especially a skill known as the "one-arm giant" that I had to preform twice around the bar. So when my coach came to me and said, "Freddy, you are done. Good job so far." I replied with, "Coach, we still have one more event to go. I can not quit!"

He said, "Even if you get on that bar and perform you would have to leave out your one-arm moves. The skills that you are doing with one arm are not going to be possible. And if you do not do those skills then the value of your routine will go down and you will not be able to get the score necessary to be placed and to rank." It is in these types of moments that you question your "why." In that moment, you question your desire to achieve.

It is very easy to let it all go and say that you are done when things get tough. How many situations in life can you relate to when you have a valid excuse and a fact that was the reason for you quitting or not taking a shot at something? How often do we use the excuse of not having had the opportunity or the chance? The excuse that if only our family was more supportive. What about the common, if I had the money excuse? We use these excuses to protect ourself by saying "It was not my fault." But, if your reasons are compelling and your "why" is strong enough then you will find all the ways that can get you closer to a winning outcome. What if you could not use the excuse card? How many of your outcomes would you have achieved by now?

Somehow, my compelling reason "why" was strong enough to get me up and on the bars. Maybe some young stupidity as well but either way my outcome outweighed the pain and potential for further injury. I was given some pain pills and massively iced my finger. The finger was then taped and stabilized to an adjacent finger. With those precautions in place, I was ready to salute and start my routine on the high bar.

Today as a medical doctor, I'm not sure if that was the wisest thing for me to do. In fact, I would probably advise myself against such behavior. The point I am trying to make however, is that when your "why" is strong and your desire is deep, nothing can stop you.

The good news is that I was able to finish my high bar routine and still include all of my one-armed moved. The bad news was that by the time I had finished and dismounted from the bar I was in tears from the sheer pain in my hand. The routine went well enough however, and I was able to place on the podium and get ranked.

From that day on, an important lesson was learned. It is something that I constantly teach my students and is valuable for anyone looking to succeed despite adversity.

> *"Nobody has any idea what is going on with you and in your life.*
> *You will only be rewarded for the outcomes you produce."*
>
> - Freddy Behin

Nobody knows the pain you are experiencing or the challenges you are currently going through. The challenges could be emotional, physical, or the lacking of resources like a broken or a missing finger. All that matters is if you have produced the results that were desired. If the results cannot be produced, you will not be rewarded. When people achieve and succeed no one knows the obstacles and challenges they had to face and to go through.

> *"You will be rewarded publicly for hours of hard work you have done in private."*
>
> - Freddy Behin

It is a natural reaction that when we hit an obstacle we use some type of an excuse to explain why we could not succeed. However, if we fail to conquer the obstacle, we come up with an excuse. It becomes the reason that stopped our success. This excuse can be a fact and the truth. But if you believe it as an absolute statement then you will never be able to succeed beyond that belief. All we are doing at that point is providing a reason for our failure so we can ultimately say, "this was not my fault." I could have easily told people that, "I would have been the champion had I not broken my finger." I also could have used the true statement that, "If my coach would not have stopped me, I would have won the Championship."

There are always excuses and true statements and facts that we can use to say why it was not our fault. But for a moment let's imagine what life would be like if all excuses in life were removed. What if you could not use any excuses from your past? Where would you be? How would your life have been? Would you have achieved the many milestones that you wish you had but for one reason or another you gave up on?

We must take responsibility for our actions and always remember that it is the actions that produce results. Every action produces a specific result and ironically, the lack of action also produces a result.

At the end of this chapter I want to leave you with the concept that you must find a way to get excited about what you are doing. Get excited for success instead of looking for obstacles. Focus on the end result and find your compelling reason "why" success is an absolute must. Your "why" will change the results of your life and make you succeed on your journey.

What gifts will you receive from this journey? Ultimately, how will these gifts help millions of other people, or even your immediate family?

Take a step forward, even if it is only one step. As long as you stay excited, you can take a step forward. The moment you lose your excitement and the reason "why" no longer becomes compelling; you need to wheel yourself to move forward. Don't stop! Stay excited and keep taking steps down your journey to achieve your *im*possible dreams.

"Your life is designed to give you the exact results you are getting today, because it is designed to do so.
Your life's design, like a formula, will reproduce these expected results.
Therefore, if you want to change the results you must change the design."

- Freddy Behin

STORY ABOUT FEAR & DECISION

I'm at a competition and I am very nervous about a skill that I must perform on the high bar. If I miss the bar I could potentially get seriously injured. In my mind I am going through an internal struggle. The struggle is to make a decision whether to perform this skill or not.

A famous boxer once said, "before you enter the ring you have already made a decision whether you are going to win or lose." I finally made the decision in my mind that I was going to overcome any insecurity or uncertainty about this move and perform the skill within my routine. Essentially, I decided that I was going to become fully committed to performing it.

My friend Brian Tracy once told me that, "…all strategies are great until you get punched in the face for the first time. Strategies are only good as long as everything goes smoothly. When things change, you must change."

An important growth phase happened for me at this competition. I was battling internally about this one maneuver and it just so happened that the gymnast before me performed the exact same skill. The terrifying part is that he missed the bar and wound up breaking his elbow. His miss resulted in him falling roughly twelve feet onto the ground. As the medics were attending to him, I was thinking to myself, "How in the world am I going to do this skill now? Now, I have actual proof that this is a very dangerous skill, and I can get hurt."

After they pulled this gymnast up and off the floor, I was up next. This is when I appreciate quotes like, "all strategies go out the window when you take your first punch to the face." I needed to identify a far better and more compelling reason as to why I should attempt this high bar maneuver.

How many times in your life have you been afraid or concerned about doing something? How many times have you watched someone fail at the exact same task you are about to tackle and asked yourself, "maybe this is not for me?" What about when a mentor or role model comes walking up to you and tells you that, "You know what? You should not do this, give up on your dream and give up on your hope." Of course they do not say that to keep you from your dreams, their intention is truly to keep you from getting hurt because they love you. Unfortunately, the advice you get from family and friends is not always going to serve you.

These thoughts swirl in your mind because you are trying to not risk getting hurt, both emotionally and physically. When people are asked on their deathbed what they regret the most about their lives they often say that they regret not having done something.

This is why I almost always smile when my students tell me that they are afraid of doing some skill or task that they have to do. Sure, they get annoyed with me, but I tell them that, "you must appreciate this feeling. This exciting and nervous anxiety will only be felt at this stage in your life. Once something becomes normal because you have proof that you have the ability and you are confident in what you are about to do, the fear and excitement go away. That is the beauty of this sport and the beauty of life, if you embrace the moments and the journey." I must always remind them that as they grow and mature as gymnasts that they will eventually be faced with losing that feeling. So instead of fighting it they must embrace that feeling and enjoy the process.

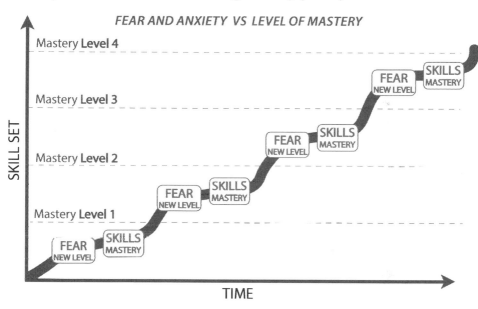

FEAR AND ANXIETY VS LEVEL OF MASTERY

This diagram demonstrates that before you gain a skill set you always have anxiety or fear. Once you achieve it and get consistent results, you no longer experience the anxiety. It simply becomes part of your belief structure and once you have accepted in your mind that you can consistently do it, you have the sense of certainty. You have moved from conscious performance mode to unconscious performance mode. You no longer have to think with high focus and precision to get results. Results just happen and you are on autopilot. This is when the excitement goes away. Which is why I remind the students to enjoy this window of opportunity and to enjoy the journey.

If you ask any high-level gymnast they will all agree with me. They will say that some of the most amazing moments that they can remember as gymnasts were moments where they experienced fear but overcame it regardless. Moments where they were truly shaken to their core but pulled it together and performed their skills. Those moments are heightened when you are successful and you say to yourself, "It actually worked!" followed by, "and I am alive!"

I have yet to find any activity in my life that closely resembles the rush you get when you feel like you are about to die but still find a way to survive, knowing that your survival was all because you committed wholeheartedly. You know you committed wholeheartedly because the slightest doubt would have thrown you off.

I absolutely love a quote that my friend Tony Robbins uses. He says, "life will give you what you ask of it. If you are asking for success, and are willing to take the risk to do what it takes, then life will reward you."

Let's get back to the story:

After about fifteen minutes of attending to the injured gymnast, they finally stabilized his elbow and moved him on a stretcher into an ambulance. This didn't change the fact that I was still performing next. I knew deep down that I would have gladly waited a few more hours, because witnessing something like that is truly terrifying.

Getting enough time for me to emotionally recover did not happen however, and I was next. The judge raised the flag and I saluted, preparing myself for what was to come next. I was raised to the high bar by my coach and began my routine. I started gaining velocity and set myself up for the skill and eventually let go of the bar. I performed my flip and twists in the air and even though it felt like I was not going to catch the bar, somehow I did. This was because I was fully committed. My hands found the bar and I was able to hold on. I was extremely nervous and excited at the same time. So much so that I could feel my muscles twitching as I was still twirling around the bar.

I finished my routine and performed my dismount. When I landed, it felt like this major weight was taken off my shoulders. At first, I was glad that I was not injured but more importantly, I was extremely happy that I was able to perform this skill that had injured the previous gymnast even though it was a skill I was not very confident about.

"Courage is being afraid, but doing it anyway!"

You see, courage is not that you are not afraid. Courage is acting despite fear. Success will throw many curve balls in your direction. There are many situations when you have to make a decision. Sometimes, these decisions can be very scary and full of risks. You could get injured, fail, become embarrassed, or lose resources but you have to commit to making a choice as well as commit to the outcome. You must find the courage to act despite fear. Also, you must learn to maintain focus on the outcome instead of the fear.

"Fear must not be fed by focusing on
what can go wrong.
Fear is starved by focusing on
what can go right."

- Freddy Behin

Your focus must stay on what actions you must take to succeed. In other words, if I am focusing on not falling I will constantly tell myself that, "I hope I don't fall, I hope I don't fall," and most likely I will fall. This is because falling was my focus. On the other hand, a small shift in my vocabulary and way of thinking leads me to say, "I will catch the bar, my hands will find the bar, I will stay focused, I will make it."

When you use the right vocabulary and the right words, your brain has to find a way to make that happen. Your focus narrows on what needs to be accomplished. Wherever your focus goes, your energy to expand it will flow. The lesson of that day was extremely profound for me. The truth of the matter was that the skill was still a dangerous skill. The important fact is that just because someone else failed at it does not mean that I will fail.

You must recognize the fact that even if others have failed before you, that does not mean that you will fail. It is moments like this where you will build the walls between yourself and your dreams. We must ensure that these moments do not allow limitations to occur on the road to living your impossible dreams. Do not let others influence you about the impossible and do not buy another person's idea that your dream is impossible. With the right mindset and focus, *im*possible is just another word, a word and concept you should recognize that shows up as an excuse to not take a shot at your dream.

Bonus Material
Action items to materialize the truth about your desire.

Download:
www.LivingImpossibleDreams.com/bonus/desire

DESIRE

CHAPTER
5

STEP-3

DECISION

"Every decision you make in life carries with it results and consequences."

- Freddy Behin

As I discussed in the previous chapter, your actions produce your results. The results either move you towards your goal and a positive outcome or they move you away. Therefore, you must take responsibility for your actions. Remember that not doing anything is also a type of action. It is the action of inaction, or not doing anything at all. This also produces results, just not positive ones. Therefore, you must take complete responsibility for both your actions as well as your inactions.

THREE CARDINAL RULES FOR SUCCESS

There are three cardinal rules in achieving success as they relate to making a decision and taking full responsibility for that decision.

You must make the decision to:

- **Rule #1** - take full responsibility for all your actions.
- **Rule #2** - do whatever it takes.
- **Rule #3** - do whatever it takes for as long as it takes.

Failing at any of these Cardinal Rules at any time, will sabotage your results. As my friend and mentor, Tony Robbins says:

*"It's in the moment of decision
that your destiny is shaped."*

- Anthony Robbins

If you entertain the concept, that all of your decisions carry with them some type of a consequence, then the consequence – which is inevitably the final result – of your decision is a reflection of the actions associated with that decision. If your decisions result in actions that will take you towards your goal then your actions ultimately produced the desired results. Understanding how you chose those decisions and what led you to make those decisions will be of great importance.

For instance, if you want to lose weight and the daily decisions you are making are not aligned with your outcome then your actions move you away from your goal. At this point most people don't take responsibility and resort to blaming their circumstances for having failed at their goal. They blame time, money and other factors for their bad decision. However if your actions align with your decision, such as eating healthy foods and leading an active lifestyle then you have made a decision to get to the outcome with the right actions.

One of the greatest oil tycoons and one of the richest self-made billionaires, Mr. Hamilton Lafayette Hunt also known as H. L. Hunt, Jr., was one of the world's richest men. He died in 1974, with a net worth of one billion dollars. He contributed his secret of success and the requirement of success to having three prerequisites.

THREE PREREQUISITES FOR SUCCESS

1. Decide what you want.
2. Determine what's the price you are willing to pay.
3. Resolve to pay the price to get what you want.

As simple as this may sound, most people fail or are unwilling to pay the price for what they want. This is especially true for the current society that we live in. We want things the easy way and are always looking for a "magic pill" to make the process easier and/or faster.

- We want our six pack abs and the perfect body.
- We want that promotion.
- We want a million dollars.
- We want that degree.
- We want that dream job.
- We want that fulfilling relationship.

For everything we want, few are willing to pay the price.

In the previous chapter we discussed the concept of desire and how it correlates to a strong and compelling "why". Your "why" is what drives you to succeed and achieve your specific goal regardless of how impossible it may seem. When you have that compelling reason, the next step is the decision. In order to achieve the desired outcome you must decide if you are willing to pay the price for it. Decide that you are willing to do whatever it takes, regardless of time or money, and take complete responsibility for all of your actions.

This step requires a massive amount of discipline because it is not easy and must be void of excuses. You cannot have any excuses or rationalizations as to why you will not pay the price. You simply must be congruent with what you want and what you are willing to do to get it done. Everyone wants to be thin, athletic and in good shape. People also want to be educated, successful, financially free and in that perfect relationship with their soul-mate. However, many refuse to pay the price required to achieve those things. If you want a great body you have to pay the price of eating healthy and exercising regularly. If you want to be successful and financially free you cannot sleep until noon every day and purchase unaffordable things on a credit card. Without discipline you will always try to do the least amount of work possible. That is not how results happen and it is not how to get the results you want.

To reiterate, we are programmed to avoid pain and discomfort while seeking pleasure. Our default mechanism is to move us towards the lowest possible discomfort level with immediate gratification. When someone does not apply discipline they will simply take the path of least resistance and revert back to their "default settings."

If you want to take over the island
you must be willing to burn the ships.

- General Hernan Cortez

One of my favorite stories is of General Hernan Cortez, one of the greatest Spanish explorers. He burnt his ships when he reached the coast of Mexico from his embarkation from Cuba in 1518. His scouts reported to him that they were outnumbered one-thousand-to-one. He faced his men and gave a loud speech as he lit the ships on fire saying, "We fight, or we die!" That was the story of the Spanish invasion of Mexico by Cortez.

The lesson here is that Cortez made a choice and decided that there was no turning back. Only victory was going to lay ahead for him. When you are so convinced about your decision that you have made and you take the right steps forward to make it a reality you remove all doubts and excuses as you move towards victory.

How many people do you know that are miserable in their job but do not move on and find a better job. How many people do you know that are unfulfilled in their relationships and are hanging on due to indecision and fear of loss. When you have one foot in and one foot out you will not go very far. You must have the desire and the ability of decision making to let go. Simply said you can not go to another room of the house unless you leave the current room.

When giving up and retreating are no longer options you will do whatever it takes to stick by your decision and make the impossible, possible.

Onc great tool that my friend and I use is public declarations and accountability. Once you make a public declaration about what you are committing to achieve, it becomes an issue of keeping your word and maintaining a high level of integrity. You must stay congruent with your identity and if you fail to follow through, your identity has been tarnished.

"Decide today that you will not settle for mediocrity or excuses and your tomorrow will be glorious."

- Freddy Behin

DECIDE TO SUCCEED

In my gymnastics career, the horizontal bars were never a comfortable event for me. Too many times, things would go wrong. The cables can snap, the grips that are holding you on the bar can rip because they are made of leather, you can slip off the bar and you can make mistakes. Any one of those incidents can result in potentially severe injuries. So, I was always uneasy about the horizontal bar.

One of the things that I love about gymnastics is that no matter how many times you have done a skill there is always a chance that you could miss. There always exists a chance that you can get hurt. No matter how many times you have done a skill perfectly, each turn and attempt is unique, requiring adjustment. These little adjustments give the view from the outside looking in the appearance that you have done it to perfection.

As you have probably seen on TV and during the Olympics or World Championships, the high bar has spectacular skills where you release the bar at a high velocity, perform flips and spins, and then re-grip the bar. Well, every time I had to do any of those release moves I had to go through a decision process. Do I let go of the bar, or hold on? And if I do let go of the bar, do I brace for a crash landing or do I go for the bar, try to catch it and potentially miss?

Of course, there are only seconds to decide and once a decision has been made, you need to stick to it and execute it all the way through. In other words, you are burning your ships.

The decision comes in two parts: Part one is to step up to the plate, part two is to actually swing. Many people step up to the plate but they freeze due to the fear of what could happen. If you do not swing, you do not get results.

Wayne Gretzky, a professional ice hockey player and known as the greatest hockey player of all times said:

"You will miss 100% of the shots you don't take."

- Wayne Gretzky

Therefore, deciding on taking the shot is a valuable step in moving towards your goal and progressing forward.

I do not think I ever felt 100% comfortable with doing my release moves on the high bar. There are so many factors that are involved in succeeding when doing a successful release move; the speed, angles, trajectory, how you physically feel as well as the responsiveness of the apparatus all play a factor in the successful execution of a skill.

A stiff bar reacts differently than a soft bar and as such you must adjust. Therefore, minor adjustments will produce different results every time. The interesting thing is when you focus on other things that can go wrong, you stop focusing on what you actually have to do to achieve greatness.

As my friend and mentor, Brian Tracy, so nicely says:

"You cannot fit two cars in a one car garage."

- Brian Tracy

Therefore, you cannot have two types of thoughts going on at the same time. You are either thinking about what can go wrong, or you are thinking about what can go right. Both options are available to you, so you must choose which thought will dominate.

When you decide to do a skill that is terrifying because something can potentially go wrong you must wholeheartedly commit yourself to it. You must focus on everything that can go right and make the decision to see it to its successful completion. There is an incredible power and energy in deciding to wholeheartedly see something succeed.

I clearly remember many competitions where I performed a skill and immediately after letting go of the bar, I knew the angle was wrong. Somehow, because I was wholeheartedly committed to ensuring that the bar would end up in my hands, those extra two or three inches required to get closer to the bar magically happened and I was able to hang on. Was it magic? All I know is that I was fully committed to achieving the skill and there was no way I was going to allow myself to slip or fall.

In summary, you must decide that you are willing to pay whatever the price is necessary for the outcome you desire. You must be willing to do whatever it takes and commit yourself wholeheartedly to see it through. You cannot hold back or cut corners, but most importantly, you must focus on everything that will go right and not what may go wrong.

Your discipline regarding this is vital. It is required so that you do not create any excuses or rationalizations and end up following the default programming for failure. Be willing to put in the work and expect nothing short of the results and success you desire. When you do what is required of you and expect the positive outcomes as a fact, you will achieve your *im*possible dreams.

Bonus Material
Action items to get you to decide wholeheartedly

Download:
www.LivingImpossibleDreams.com/bonus/decision

DECISION

CHAPTER
6

STEP-4

PLANNING

"Without a plan and a clear direction any direction and plan will sound good at the time."

- Freddy Behin

Remember that all bad ideas sounded good at one point in time, only to be discovered later that it was a bad idea. In order to prevent bad ideas you must plan before taking any action.

The planning phase is broken down into 4 steps:

1. Define your Goal and Outcome
2. Define Your Strategies
3. Model a Mentor or a Coach
4. Anticipate Setbacks

DEFINE YOUR GOAL AND OUTCOME

Most of the successful people I know are long-term thinkers. They look far into the future and identify their goals. Successful people see where they want to go, plan accordingly to achieve that goal, and work their way back to the present to identify the appropriate steps to take in order to achieve the desired success. You close this gap between where you are and where you want to go by breaking it up into manageable parts. By doing this you can make sure that every step you take is congruent with where you want to be in the future.

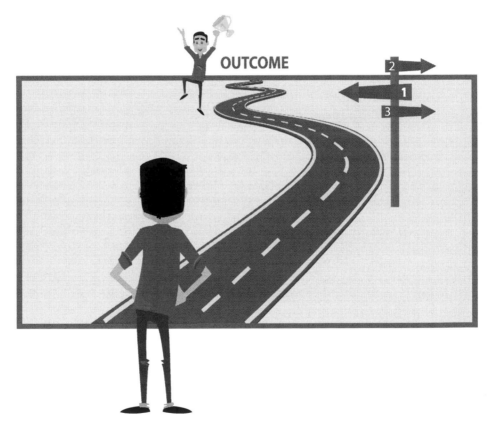

DEFINE YOUR STRATEGIES

Unless you have an accurate instruction manual you may have to learn the rules of the game through trial-and-error. The issue with trial-and-error learning is that it can take an enormous amount of time and might involve emotional, physical and/or financial setbacks.

What are the best strategies that will get you to your goal? As the old saying goes "there is more than one way to skin a cat", but there are only a few that are most efficient and less taxing on you. It is important to recognize that when you operate on only one option in life you are really left with no option and have no choice. The dilemma is that if you can not use that option you are doomed. When you only have one way to win and you hit a wall or setback, you will give up and stop searching for other solutions, because you only gave yourself one path to travel. When you operate on two or more options and choices you have ultimately given yourself the position to chose the best option and strategy for your outcome. You must find more than two options so you can weigh them against each other and pick the most effective and efficient one. As much as the saying goes that "all roads lead to Rome", you must recognize that not all roads will get there with the same ease and grace, and more importantly some roads may take way longer than necessary. Spend some effort in your planning process to pick the right road.

With efficiency you can accomplish whatever you desire faster and with more certainty. The most efficient actions with the least amount of waste in both time and resources will lead you to accomplishing your goals much faster. If your goal has the potential for physical, emotional or financial risks, you must take whatever measures are necessary to prevent yourself from experiencing those risks.

It's wise to discover the best model or path to your goal. Out of multiple options available choose only actions that have a low risks factor and minimal rate for failure and/or injury. More specifically, you must stay in the game to win. The model that best suits you is always the one that will make sure you are getting to your goal effectively and at the same time allowing you to "live to fight another day." You must identify by what path or manner your actions need to be executed to achieve your goal.

MODEL A MENTOR OR A COACH

The common pattern in those who are successful is that during their planning and preparation stages they find and associate themselves with a mentor and a coach. These people find out what successful people who have already succeeded in reaching similar goals have done. To be a successful learner you must study under those who are accomplishing what you also want to accomplish. Seek mentors and coaches who are consistently getting the results and achieving their results over and over again.

For example, if you want to increase your finances by learning about finance, you must seek out someone who is already financially successful. The last thing you want to do is take advice from friends who arc financially unsuccessful. You want to model yourself after someone who is already succeeding.

All too often I see instructors who try to teach health and fitness while they are not healthy. The best thing you can do for yourself is to choose a teacher, instructor or mentor who has set high standards for efficiency and proficiency. Seek out someone who is already at a high level of success and is living the life that you wish to live. Those are the people you need to model yourself after. The critical importance of this step means that you will find instructors who do not have limitations on growth. When you are looking at someone who is not healthy themselves and they have limitations in their belief system on how healthy they can be, you will adopt the same self-limiting mindset and the same self-limiting belief system that you learncd from them.

ANTICIPATE SETBACKS

Setbacks can be a normal part of the process or a feedback for you that you must make changes to get different results.

Your ability to identify these setbacks as normal or pathological will have a major impact on your ability to continuc the process or fall in the category of those who say "I tried but I hit a bump on the road and that is why I gave up". Let me give you an example.

When you go to the gym after a long time off and train very hard to cover for lost time you will have a resulting setback the next few days. The setback shows up as you being sore and not being able to do the same exercise you did. As a matter of fact you seem to have lost strength and mobility. Does that mean you should not workout again since you're actually worse off now? Is this a pathological setback or a normal sctback? However if you recognize that afler not having worked out for a while and going to the gym at the same intensity as before, you will have this type of setback. You will not be surprised when the setback occurs. You will be able to anticipate the actions you must take in order to avoid the setback altogether or be able to plan for it. In this workout example you could be doing a low intensity workout for a few days before you actually go all out. That allows your body to turn on first instead of the over stressing your body. Or the other option would be, deal with the muscular fatigue and use the next few days to do activities that do not involve the intense use of those muscles, such as stretching, yoga or swimming. Again, understanding that there is a recovery period as the muscle rebuilds itself will allow you to understand that you actually do not have a setback and this is a normal process.

However if you have been going to the gym and all of a sudden you feel fatigued and/or feel a loss of strength, you must look at it as a feedback, since that is not a normal result. At this point you must check for nutrition, physical health and sleep patterns etc. Since this is not a normal setback you use the feedback to discover new actions. In other words just because you hit a low does not mean that you are failing. Ask yourself, is this an anticipated setback or is it telling me that I need to make changes? Do not feel as you have failed, when a setback is expected. Anticipate these patterns of setbacks and embrace them by planning to deal with them.

In summary, during your planning phase you must have the end in mind. Be clear and specific about what it is that would be considered a win for you. Next, you want to find several options and strategies by which you can get there. With only one choice you will be limited and in case of a small setback you might be out of options. In order to find multiple options and strategies you must associate yourself with mentors and coaches who have gone through this path successfully and consistently. You must recognize that every path has potential for moments of setbacks. Some setbacks are an expected part of the process and some are there to give you warnings and feedback to make changes. Anticipate them and have plans to deal with them. With the clear goal in your mind and a map filled with multiple options giving you flexibility on your journey with many detours, you will be sure to move towards your goal without the distractions of setbacks as a signal that you should abandon the journey altogether. Many quit just inches away from success not realizing that their next attempt would have given them the breakthrough.

Bonus Material
Action material to clarify your planning process.

Download:
www.LivingImpossibleDreams.com/bonus/plan

PLAN

CHAPTER
7

STEP-5

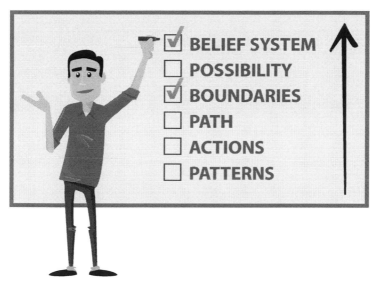

PREPARATION

*"Give me six hours to chop down a tree and
I will spend the first four sharpening the axe"*

- Abraham Lincoln

Once you have made the right planning you will need to prepare mentally and internally.

The preparation phase is broken down into 3 steps:

1. Your Belief System
2. Design Your Path
3. Discover Your Patterns

YOUR BELIEF SYSTEM

Once you have made the conscious decision that you are fully committed to your goal, it is vital that you are aware of your belief system around this goal. Your ability to see the possibilities versus the obstacles is vital to achieving your outcomes. Your ability to see a solution or at least entertain that there is one when you hit a dead end is what makes the difference. We all have a belief system around our abilities and limitations. Expanding those beliefs will give you the tools that will trump any talent. This imaginary boundary around your abilities will stop you from crossing to the other side. If I asked you how much is a lot of money and what you think you could make this year, you would respond based on your reality and boundary limits. It is only when you expand that boundary that living on the other side of it is a reality. Your belief system has valid facts to ensure you that those boundaries exist for a reason. They are simply excuses for you not to cross over. Even if you try and you fail, those facts are there for you to hold on to as an excuse to ultimately say it was not your fault and because of these facts you could not move past the boundary. I must remind you again, this is an imaginary boundary. You are the only one that sees it and has the ability to expand it.

As you work your way outside of the boundaries, be sure you are taking the right steps towards success. Do not get caught up saying "but I am working so hard". You need to work right instead. Doing the right thing, in the right sequence and at the right time. You must learn the rules of the game. Once you do that, you simply have to play the game harder than anyone else around you.

Even if the goal or target you are aiming for seems impossible, you must focus your desires and intentions to find that one possibility that makes your dreams come true. There is always a way to succeed and there is always a way to find it. If you are in the mindset that everything is rigged against you and there are no possibilities, then your mind will do everything in its power to keep you congruent with that thought and you will attract a sequence of events that will lead you to that belief and corresponding outcome. You will then get the reinforcement of that negative belief and say,

"See? I knew it wouldn't work. I tried so hard. I worked so hard."
We are very clever organisms and our brains, when posed with a
question or a fact, will search for an answer through the filter that
it has created. That filter is your belief system. When you naturally
believe you are a lucky person, you will find ways to be lucky. When
you feel like the world is against you and you are always unlucky,
guess what happens to you? You must choose and develop a
belief system that will serve you.

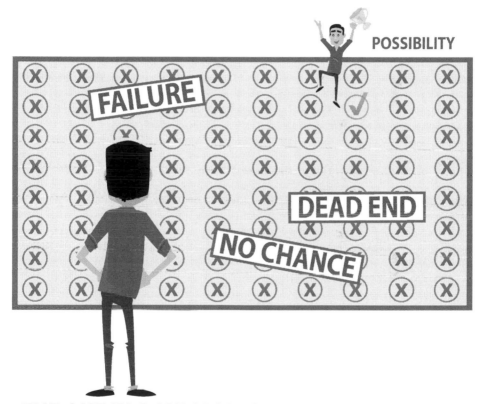

THE ONE IN A MILLION CHANCE

Personally, I love comedy. I truly believe that laughter and comedy
are the necessities of life. One of my favorite movies in the mid-90s
was "Dumb and Dumber" with Jim Carrey. There was a profound
scene in this movie where Jim Carrey is trying to find the love of
his life. This is someone that he fell in love with from a one time

chance meeting while giving her a ride to the airport. He travels across the country despite not knowing her name or where she is staying. Against all challenges and odds and with only one focus on his mind, he finally gets the chance to meet her.

At last, when they meet he finds the strength and the courage to ask her if her feelings are reciprocated. He encourages her to answer honestly and simply asks, "What are my chances with you?" To his surprise the answer was, "Not very good." After a slight pause he reflects on the situation and says, "Not very good as in...one-in-one-hundred?" The lady responds with, "More like one-in-a-million." After another slight pause and with a puzzled look he searches for the meaning of what just happened. Suddenly, he becomes extremely excited and jumps for joy! He responds with, "So you are telling me that there is a chance! Yeah!!!"

I simply love this scene. Not only for the comedic action of it but also for the message that is communicated to the world. I'm sure many people have missed that message; that even if there is a one-in-a-million chance, there is still a chance.

You can focus on the million different ways that you are unable to achieve your goal or you can focus on the one way that leads to success. Again, this is the reason why finding mentors and teachers to look up to is important. They are the ones who have achieved that one-in-a-million. They will tremendously shape the way you think about your potential and possibility of winning. It will also shorten the time that it takes for you to achieve whatever you desire.

DESIGN YOUR PATH

Regardless how complicated and how difficult an outcome might be, you must learn to break it down into segments. Each segment will have its own segments and ultimately you will discover that there are measurable chunks of steps and sequences that will make an apparently complicated and intricate outcome come to life.

You become a doctor, engineer, accountant or any other profession you can think of simply one step at a time. You get there by completing one day, one class, one exam and one assignment at a time. Therefore every step counts and every step is vital. The beauty here is that when you only look at that one class, one day, or that one exam, your task does not seem that overwhelming. When you see a champion, they did not just end up being a champion. Their journey was also one day at a time, one injury at a time and one overcoming of fear and doubt at a time that created the champion. Often we give up on our goal because the big goal and outcome seems too far to achieve. But when we only focus on one tiny step and only focus on getting that one step done, we build on our success and enjoy the journey while we get closer and closer to the ultimate goal.

DISCOVER YOUR PATTERNS

We all have patterns for our life on what we do, why we do it and how we do it. The consistency in our patterns is based on our desire to protect ourselves and our need to develop a consistency in our emotions and how we feel. To achieve the feeing of safety and security we behave a certain way and to achieve a desired emotional state we behave accordingly. The scope of the psychology and human behavior that is related to this topic is another book by itself so we will keep it short here. However the idea is that we all have a system that we have adopted as a system that we believe works for us and gives us the desired results. I call these your natural patterns. These patterns are based on your values and belief systems. You use these in all areas of your life however you are not aware of them as they are unconscious to you.

For example you may have a pattern of trying something three times before you start feeling that it is not working and letting go of it. That may have caused you to missed out on the success that you could have experienced on the forth try but you never experienced it because your natural behavior always distracted you away after the third attempt. Another example could be that whenever you have too many important things to do, you get overwhelmed. Your pattern then would be to start organizing and spending too much time obsessing about what is priority and what is not, instead of simply taking imperfect actions you windup not even getting started. Precisely because the priority on all items were high and you just freeze and don't get anything done. What about when you get stressed? What type of patterns do you have that don't serve you? Do you reach for food or get caught up in social media and TV for hours?

If you recognize these patterns that run your life and cause you to take action or avoid actions, you can reproduce them when you need them or anticipate and conquer them if they do not serve you. These patterns are also easily recognizable in your physiology and biochemistry of your body and they are very predictable.

"Imperfect actions consistently taken trumps all perfect actions never taken"

- Freddy Behin

Let me tell you about my journey to the Gymnastics World Championship and how this concept played a vital role.

When I was training for the World Championships I had a training schedule that was planned eleven months in advance. When you do something like that you must have the end goal in mind. As

Stephen Covey says, "Start with the end in mind." Ironically, when I made my training schedule I did not know about Stephen Covey but it seemed like we were aligned in our thinking.

I started with the day of the competition, when the World Championships would occur, and worked backwards from there for eleven months. I knew that by April 15th I needed to be at the best shape of my entire life. I needed to be ready to compete and not be exhausted, injured or weak. Everything had to come together on that specific day.

People think that you can just keep training and condition yourself in order to be strong by a certain date. The reality is that your body goes through phases. It goes through cycles of peaks and valleys and if you do not allow it to rest, your body can enter deterioration mode when you need it to be in perfect condition instead. Therefore, you must work backwards so you can listen to your body and recognize these cycles.

When I developed this plan eleven months earlier I was able to see all the patterns my body was going through. When my body was at its strongest I correlated it with the type of conditioning and exercises I had to do. I also added a nutritional diet as part of that plan.

The truth is that we are not like computers or machines. Each system of our body including digestion, metabolism, etc. and their recovery times are all different.

Each one of us has a different pattern. The key is to discover what your pattern is, how your body recovers, how your body conditions, how many days are required in between and what type of diet works for you. Another important part of this preparation was the periods when I had to do the grinding work. The periods when I needed to deliver quality. In other words, there were days where I had to do a certain number of repetitions and it did not matter what the quality of them were. I know this will sound like a contradiction to what I said earlier about working smarter and my accuracy level of doing things being at 100% but accuracy is not the same as conditioning your body and building reflexes for repetitive actions. Which is the reason unconscious competency develops, where you do things without having to over think and focus. I will describe that more in the next chapter.

Back to the plan and the patterns. So you exhaust yourself on days where you just do repetitions, over and over again. Then you have days when you perform for quality. You only have one or two attempts but they absolutely must be perfect.

"Train as if you are competing and compete as if you are training."

-Freddy Behin

There is so much truth to that.

I catch many of the students that I train saying, "Oh, I messed up. That was just a warm-up." My response is always, "Your warm-up should be your best effort." You are warming up what you will perform, it should be warming up the perfect results not a portion of it.

Again the purpose of me doing this process was to be clear about how my body reacts based on the training type, nutrition, stress etc. By knowing how I react and respond and finding my personal pattern I was able to manufacture the level of fitness and accuracy I needed for my competition day. We have the same pattern in our business lives and personal relationship lives. We react a certain way when challenges occur and sometimes our reaction is not favorable to what will get us to the desired outcome. If you recognize your patterns that serve you and are favorable, you can do more of them. Conversely, recognizing and managing the patterns that do not serve you, will also allow you to work around them so you do not fail. Understanding these patterns will give you a clear path to your outcome.

In this chapter we discovered the mental aspect of preparation. You must recognizing that you have an imaginary wall that you impose on yourself based on your belief system. You have to be able to see yourself outside of that wall and see the possibility.

You must find that one specific way those things are possible instead of focusing on a million ways that you could fail. Focus on that one chance that could give you victory.

Your ability to create a plan based on the multiple options you have discovered in the last chapter is vital to get you to know in small steps what has to happen every day, while being focused on the outcome. When you have a plan of action on the daily and weekly basis you are not overwhelmed by the ultimate outcome. Your task is only one or two vital actions every day. While going through your plan you must take note of natural patterns that you possess. Take note of patterns that make things easier and patterns that set you back. Once you recognize those triggers you can intentionally trigger them for the desired results.

Bonus Material
Action material to clarify your preparation process.

Download:
www.LivingImpossibleDreams.com/bonus/prep

PREP

CHAPTER
8

STEP-6

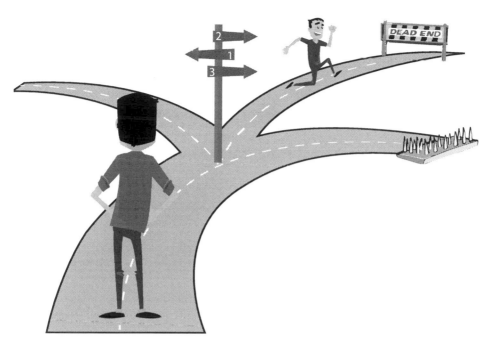

WORK

DO THE RIGHT WORK

*"No matter how long and how fast you have been going
on the wrong road, stop and turn back.
The person that stops and goes back is ahead.
Not the other way."*

- Freddy Behin

"No matter how long you have been going on the wrong road, turn back. Don't be busy on the wrong road, going the wrong direction! The person that stops and goes back is ahead of you, not the other way."

There is a universal law of cause and effect. For every action there is a reaction or result. You have to make sure that you are taking the right steps to produce the right results for your outcome.

It is not enough for you to just do the work to get you to the outcome. You must do the right work. I know this may sound like it is common sense, but you will be surprised how many people actually expect results by doing the wrong work and as a result windup give up on their quest, because they don't see results. You must commit to consistently do the right work at each step of the process.

Ask yourself: "What is that one crucial component that makes all the difference?"

Luckily there is a trick and a tool that will help you with those questions.

THE POWER OF ONE - 80/20/1 RULE

As you are planning it is important to pay attention to the idea of "smart work". You have to work smart. What I mean by this is that not all effort is equally rewarded. You might be able to get the same exact result by doing something that is more effective and less time consuming. You might be able to save a great deal of pain by doing the right work. Consider what the right work is and resolve to complete and execute it diligently.

Eliminate all inefficiencies and get straight to the point. Only perform tasks and activities that will allow you to take steps closer to your positive outcome and eliminate activities that will not get you to where you want to be. Focus only on the work that will give you the maximum positive result.

I like to refer to this as the 80/20/1 rule. In general, there are 20% of the tasks that will give you more than 80% of the results. You want to focus on that 20% first.

There are three steps involved in the 80/20/1 rule that you should master:

1. Identify your **GOAL** - What is it that truly matters to you?
2. Identify your **ROUTE** - What is the most effective path?
3. Identify your **ACTION** - What is the most effective execution?

Essentially: Identify what you want, how to get it, and the best method of attaining it. In the process of all this, do the work and be as efficient about it as possible. On many occasions when you get to the 20% you may still be overwhelmed with actions that you have to take. Sometimes the overwhelm of many action causes paralysis in taking action in the first place and not knowing where to start.

The way to deal with this challenge is simply by continuing the 80/20/1 rule into a narrow funnel until you get to a handful of actions that are ranked in priority and order.

Now simply ask yourself which items are the tasks that will give you the most effective results, but then ask yourself if you could not do them all and only had to choose one task, which one would give you the most results and satisfaction? That must become your #1 priority and must get your full presence. You must put all your focus on this item to be done accurately and completely. Only then you can move to the next item that would give the next highest result. By doing this you avoid the major pitfall of not taking action due to the overwhelm of information, choices and tasks, but instead focus on the most important task that gives you the best results. That is why I call this a 80/20/1 rule.

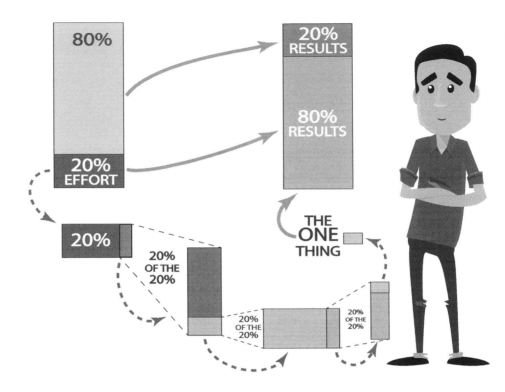

In the previous chapter, I spoke about making decisions and ensuring that they are made wholeheartedly. This however, does not mean to make those decisions wholeheartedly and carelessly. I would like to share again one of my greatest experiences as a high-level gymnast.

If you recall, an injury to my finger almost wiped me out from placing at the national level after a year of training. The same is true for many great athletes who never make it to the championships in their sport due to injury. Although injuries do happen, you can prevent them by preparing in the right way. By anticipating and taking calculated risks, many injuries can be prevented through proper planning and preparation.

As a gymnast, I had many training days where I trained myself without a spotter. Although there was always a coach around, their actual presence and dedication was questionable and I had to rely on myself. Having a coach physically present most of the time decreases the potential for injury when performing high-level skills that might harm you. You especially have to be careful if you are performing them by yourself.

One of these skills is a double-flip with a completely straight body on the floor exercise. We call that skill a "Double Back Laid Out", or in gymnastics lingo and terms, a "Double Lay". In order to achieve this skill you must have a lot of speed as well as enough suspension and height to accomplish two revolutions with a straight body. You must punch extremely hard off the tumbling floor which puts tremendous pressure on your ankles and Achilles tendon. At the same time, your heels absorb an immense amount of pressure on the landing. If you land short of your target or at the wrong angle, your tendons can become severed.

A part of doing the right work and being efficient is also being smart and not getting hurt. I spent a long time doing prep work on skills that would lead up to the actual Double Lay without actually performing the skill. I would simulate rotations and I would practice skills that lead up to the Double Lay to generate greater speed. These were called "round-off back handsprings." I would practice these over and over with perfect accuracy. I would practice this sometimes for 30 minutes straight instead of working on the Double Lay for that same amount of time. This helped keep pressure off my ankles. I would also do all the mental prep work for 20-30 minutes and visualize myself performing the Double Lay repeatedly until perfection. When I was satisfied with the visual result I would attempt the skill between three to five times only.

The lesson here, is that when I did those skills, for only three to five tries and did them flawlessly or as we call it when I "nailed them" three to five times, my accuracy level was at a 100%. In other words if I do that only three times and I finish it perfectly three times in a row and stopped there, I have had a 100% accuracy.

I could have done it the other way where I performed the skill 30 times and only landed it perfectly ten times. Not only did I have an accuracy level of 33% but I also would put tremendous pressure on my body and potentially injure myself.

Simply put, how many turns and tries does it take you to get something perfect? What if you could get your mind so prepared that you get the perfect results every single time? You have to be able to deliver your results consistently and when it matters. It only counts when it is consistent and it only matters when it gets you to your desired outcome. Doing it perfectly when you are being evaluated is when it matters to be consistent.

How often have you done the busy work and achieved poor results in life? The length of time and number of turns does not always equal the result.

The right work in the most efficient way possible while avoiding pain is the key to doing your planning. You want to "live to fight another day" and still increase your efficiency level so that you can achieve positive results more often.

Another aspect is the mental capacity and self-esteem that comes with an accuracy rating of 100% versus 33%. My confidence level was much higher when I accomplished the skill 100% of the time. It let me know that when the time arrived that I need to perform, I could successfully achieve that skill exactly the way I imagined it. I was in control. Knowing this allowed me to dedicate myself to it wholeheartedly.

Doing the 80/20/1 rule requires an understanding of who the top performers are and what skill they have acquired while knowing the distinction that helped them achieve it. When looking at a task, there are many components that can be tackled and many aspects that all need attention.

If you could only pick one area to focus on, what would it be? What would be that one "thing" that would give you the most results? Also, once you have preplanned ideas, you practice diligently, over and over until you achieve the mastery level at which you can perform unconsciously.

In a sport like gymnastics, you are not able to retain all of the technical aspects of the skill all at once. When you are doing a complicated skill you are not thinking about all of the individual motions or every single thing that must happen in order for that skill to be accomplished. Our brains do not process fast enough to digest all that information and pass the right signals back to your muscles to perform at that speed. However, because of the practice that you have repeatedly done you have developed a reflex. That is why I use the 80/20/1 rule.

Ask yourself, "What is the one thing that I need to be maintaining in my mind while my body does the rest of the reflex?" Or, "What is the one thing that I need to be doing differently that would make this an accomplished skill?" That's why I repeatedly spent thirty minutes doing all the mental prep work. This was so my body remembers the reflex automatically. When I am ready to attempt the skill my mind works with only that one distinction that will make the skill successful.

Of course, I am not just talking about gymnastics. Whatever the skill is, you would perform the same process. Relationships are the same as well. Ask yourself this, "Specifically, what is the one thing I could be doing that will have the most positive impact on my health, finances and relationships?" It is very important that you have a plan and that your plan covers you from the start of your journey all the way to the end result.

FOUR STAGES OF COMPETENCE

When we strive for competency in any area of life, such as business, finances, health, athletics or a new hobby, we all go through the same process.

When we are introduced to something new and a new skill much like watching the Olympics and wanting to be an Olympian the next day by joining a gym and buying shiny new uniforms we are inspired and at the first stage.

Noel Burch discovered a model for learning any new skill back in 1970s. He categorized the process of learning in four stages.

UNCONSCIOUS INCOMPETENCE

You have the wrong intuition about the process and reality. You do not understand or know how to do something and do not necessarily recognize the deficits you may have. You may even deny the usefulness of the new skill. At this stage you are lacking the knowledge and the skill-set. The length of time an individual spends in this stage depends on the how long they stay inspired and stimulated.

CONSCIOUS INCOMPETENCE

At this stage you recognize the reality and usefulness of the skill-set and you realize that you are lacking the skills and competency. You do not know how to perform yet and do not understand why. This is the moment when you go through trial and error to see what works. This is the stage that you have to actually do work and you realize that the work is not easy, fun or painless. Your length of stay in this stage depends on how willing you are to learn the skill-set and how you deal will failure. This is the stage that most people give up and if they do not get the results will label themselves or others as not talented or say this is not for me.

CONSCIOUS COMPETENCE

At this stage you know enough to know what needs to be done. You understand and know how to do something. However doing so requires your focus and concentration. Since you understand the process and have gained the power to correctly analyze you are able to achieve results with relative consistency.

UNCONSCIOUS COMPETENCE

At this stage you have done the skill enough times that it has become a habit for you. The fact that you had so much practice with the skill allows it to become "second nature" and can be performed easily. This is why you are able to perform this skill while executing another task. You have a very high rate of consistency and can teach it to others as well.

INSTANT GRATIFICATION DISEASE

One of the major challenges in our current life time is exponential growth of technology, communication and cell phones. Due to the responsiveness of the technology and the way we now communicate or browse the Internet or watch shows on demand and instantaneously, we have lower attention spans. As a matter of fact we have dropped 50% within the last decade alone. According to a research done by Microsoft Corporation, the ability of humans to multi task has increased but our attention span has dropped lower than a goldfish. Humans now have an attention span of 8 seconds versus the 9 second attention span of a goldfish.

The challenge with this loss of attention span is that we are no longer able to delay gratification. If we do something we expect immediate results. If the results are not produced immediately we lose attention and interest.

So when people get to the Conscious Incompetence and do not have the results immediately, they lose focus and their attention goes somewhere else. Unfortunately, it is at this point where most people give up on their dreams. They will attempt their dreams and because they fail to achieve immediate gratification and success they will believe that they are not capable of achieving their goals. They revert back to excuses and justifications for failure. They say, "this is too hard." or, "I am not talented enough." and feel that they were not given the right resources or were just "not lucky."

Remember, you must be willing to pay the price that is asked of you, to gain what you want. That means you must be willing to do the work regardless of how long the process is or how difficult it becomes. You must be committed and your commitment must be so strong that you will not stop moving forward. Check your plan, adjust accordingly and continue to take another step forward.

Thomas Edison reportedly tried over ten thousand different ways to get the light bulb to work. He tried over ten thousand different substances to create the filament necessary for the light bulb to function. When he was asked by a reporter, "What do you think about your failures during those ten thousand attempts?" he replied that, "I do not look at them as failures. I have found over ten thousand ways how the light bulb does not work." This led him to his ten thousandth and ninth attempt where he was finally able to find the right substance to make the light bulb illuminate. Thomas Edison has over a thousand different patents under his name and forever became known as a man who would never give up.

How many people give up after the first 10 attempts? How about how many people give up after 100 attempts, or even 1000? Edison was successful because he was committed. He was successful because his mindset was focused on the outcome. He was able to do that because he knew that there had to be a way to succeed. His desire led him to make a decision, planned for his success, and then did the work no matter the price.

Another great example is Michael Jordan. One of the greatest basketball players of all time, Michael Jordan has lost over three hundred games. He has missed over nine thousand shots and when he was given the ball during the last second to make the winning shots, he lost over twenty-six games. Michael Jordan also believed that every time he missed a shot, he learned something from it. Because of this, his basketball game became stronger and more resilient. That is why he is one of the best players ever known. He learned by missing over nine thousand shots.

Remember, you will miss 100% of the shots you do not take.

Let's review this chapter: You must do the right work. You will know what the right work is when you find the right people that are already doing it and living it.

You must be efficient. Find out what that one significant step is that you must take. A significant step that when taken will give you maximum results.

Always remember the 80/20/1 rule. Of course, keep yourself from getting injured but again, we are not talking about gymnastics. We are talking about life. An injury can occur when you break up in a relationship because you made the wrong move. An injury can occur when you make the wrong investment and your money is gone. Avoid getting injured.

So, when you are doing a "Double Lay" in life you have to make sure that you are nailing it three out of three times; every single time.

As a side note, I want to remind you that there will always be others around you that will focus on the many ways that you can fail. In many ways these people may not mean to cause harm. They may just want to protect you from getting hurt. Remember we all have a belief system and limitations in our belief system that create an imaginary boundary of possibilities around us. You must be careful believing what they say because if there is a one-in-a-million chance…you must strive for the *im*possible.

Bonus Material
Diagram on how DIP and progress work.

Download:
www.LivingImpossibleDreams.com/bonus/work

WORK

CHAPTER
9

STEP-7

EVALUATION

"What you measure can be brought to life and controlled. What gets controlled will deliver consistency."

- Freddy Behin

When we first learn how to ride a bicycle, our movements are not very smooth. When we make corrections we tend to over-correct and as a result we sway from side-to-side. When we have more time on the bicycle and spend more time correcting our mistakes we soon realize that the sudden movements are not necessary. Eventually, we have a minuscule number of adjustments that permit us to ride straight. Even the best cyclists in the world have to make adjustments as they are riding. However, their adjustments are so tiny that they are not easily visible by the naked eye.

In order for you to consistently deliver the best results you must learn what the needed adjustments are. To do that, you actually need to fail. Without failure you have no experience as to what types of adjustments need to be made. Every time you make an attempt you must stop and recognize what did and did not work so you can evaluate and make adjustments to your strategy so that you succeed next time. If things do not work out for you then you must go back to the previous step and find out from others who know better than you. These people have produced the results that you are seeking to achieve so they can help you find ways to make your strategy work for you. You need to learn which crucial step you may have missed so that it can be corrected.

There are times that you feel that the results are not as smooth as you'd like or that you are putting in more effort than the results that are being produced.

The truth is that progress is not a linear process. You do not consistently grow and achieve results. You will hit plateaus and peaks as well as valleys. When you hit a plateau, that means that if you do not change or make adjustments, you will stay there. There is a great saying, "what got you here will not get you there." What this means is that when you hit a plateau it is because of your current amount of knowledge, resources and abilities being perfectly tailored for exactly where you are at. In order to break through beyond the plateau you must first evaluate the situation, improve your abilities and then change or make modifications to your plan. Sometimes the setbacks take a while to persevere through but these will happen until you perfect what you are doing and become proficient at making adjustments consistently.

When you show progress as we discussed in Chapter Two, you will take more action. When you hit a decline in progress however, it can feel similar to achieving little to no results. What happens is that most people drop out of the race at this point or they set themselves back into their last plateau.

Sometimes this is the only thing that separates those who succeed at a high level from those who are just blending in with the average player. For those who persevere through plateaus and decline and do whatever it takes to break through, there is good news awaiting you. Typically, breaking through a plateau leads to another major spike in progress and achievement. This opens a whole new set of possibilities and accomplishments that were previously more difficult to obtain.

Now you will have a different level of consciousness and a different level of self-esteem as well as a different level of skill than what you had previously. What was once unachievable has now become a possibility. You must understand that progress requires plateaus and setbacks and those are a regular part of progress. Without having these difficulties there would be little information on how to improve yourself and your ability to reach for impossible dreams.

The way I like to look at setbacks and failure is that they are a feedback mechanism. When I fail, I have simply discovered a way that does not work for me. It is also a feedback mechanism when I have hit a plateau and can no longer progress towards my goals. I am getting the feedback required to adjust and create new skill sets. Evaluate and try to understand what went wrong and continuously make adjustments to try again.

Remember as things become harder and challenges occur you must go back to step one and re-evaluate. Make sure that your mindset is still correct and that you have not adapted to any self-limiting beliefs. You must make certain that you have not adopted other people's self-limiting beliefs as well. Also, re-evaluate your desire and the strength of your "why" to be clear that you are truly committed to the decision you have made. Re-evaluate if you are doing the right work and if you are being efficient at it.

Success is only possible if you can have the discipline and overcome the natural tendencies most humans have to cut corners on. Over 80% of successful people in business, finance, athletics and show business have the same thing in common. What they have in common is that they are willing to work harder than anyone else in their field. Hard work is the key to creating lasting success and is only available to you if you truly are willing to do the work.

THE ILLUSION OF PERFECTION

I am always intrigued when people ask or tell me about the perfection that a gymnast shows on an apparatus. They see gymnasts do skills and they appear flawless to them. As a matter of fact, it looks like nothing is going wrong. The truth is that a good gymnast who has done the work and has gone through the setbacks and plateaus understands how to make adjustments as a reaction to compensate. When we see a flawless routine it is actually the gymnast doing many adjustments in order for it to be perfect when seen by others.

If the gymnast is over-rotating, they will kick out earlier. If a gymnast is under-rotating they will hang on tighter. Gymnasts kick harder when they are too slow and also stretch out when they need to slow the routine down. The result of all of these small adjustments is that others will see a perfect routine.

The fact is that those little adjustments can occur because you have experienced them before. If you are caught with a surprise then you would not know what to do to mitigate the change and you will crash. So, the more work you have done and the more plateaus you have broken through the more likely you are to make the small adjustments necessary to create a flawless result. At least from an outsider's perspective it will appear flawless but to you and I, we now know that there are small corrections being made along the way.

This is also why it is very important to have gone through the process of anticipating setbacks. You can recognize changes by getting feedback and evaluating the solution for the next step. When you know what can go wrong and you have made plans for that instant and have practiced it, you will not be surprised. When something goes wrong you move to plan A, B, C and if necessary even plan D.

FINDING YOUR MENTOR

Remember, you have to search for a mentor who is producing the results over and over again consistently. Those are the people you must look for. And, if need be, you can use them as your coaches. Use those who are achieving the results over and over in a consistent manner and use them as your mentors and coaches.

Very often we are unable to see our own blind spots. However, someone who is producing the results we wish to achieve is able to identify flaws in our execution. That is what makes them perfect people to review your progress and see where distinctions occur between your plan and theirs. This can sometimes help you break out of a low progression cycle or move beyond plateaus. The key aspect that you have to remember at all times while being evaluated and working towards progress is that you are constantly taking one forward step after another. You absolutely must not stop taking action.

You recognize that this is the price that you must pay in order to achieve greatness. As long as you are moving forward, you are in the game. If you have ever tried to lose weight, or if you have already lost some weight but hit a plateau, you must recognize what is taking place. The same applies for a financial plateau where your income level is not changing as quickly as you would like it to. Always remember that what got you to where you are is not what is going to get you to the next level.

What you must do is look for what you are not seeing. You must search for what needs to change, search for what you must add to your skill set or resources as well as what it is that separates you from the people who are achieving the success you desire.

Growth is always related to change. If you are not willing to make the necessary changes then you will not surpass what you already know. Therefore, when you hit a plateau you must listen and be aware of the feedback that you are getting from those who are successful around you. You must discover what changes you must make and then relentlessly do that work to get the results you desire. This is what moves you beyond the plateau phase.

Remember that success always leaves clues.

If you do what successful people do consistently, you will be able to enjoy the same results and rewards. However, if you ignore what successful people do then you will have less of a chance of being successful. In other words, do more of what works and do less of what does not work. Success is predictable and is not often found by accident. Equally, failure is not an accident either.

WATCH YOUR WORDS

One of the greatest harms that we as adults do to young children are to program their minds that failure is not a good thing. We teach them that if they fail that they have done something wrong and they will spend the rest of their lives trying to figure out ways to prevent failure. In the process of doing so they learn to avoid challenges that could potentially cause them to fail.

As adults we program the minds of children on what they are gifted at based on how fast they achieve competency. We also program their minds that if they take too long in reaching competency they should not engage in the activity since it is wasting their time. they should engage in activities they naturally succeed at.

The most successful people have failed numerous times and used their failure as stepping stones to success. That is how they have improved themselves. Every time they failed they looked for a better way to succeed or an alternative path to success while looking back and assessing what parts of their plan worked and what did not.

We have to get over the thought that if we fail we look bad to our peers or that we will be judged by those around us. The reality is that everyone has their own journey. We all have our own path towards progress filled with peaks and valleys that occur based on what we have previously done.

If you invest the time and you have paid the price then you will experience better results and your progress will continue for a longer time before hitting the inevitable plateau in your journey. If you have cut corners or looked for shortcuts on the journey to success then your progress will stall and you will hit the plateau much sooner. Therefore, progress and growth both require a certain degree of failure.

When people refer to someone as an expert what we are really saying is that they have experienced failure so many times that they now know how to get out of any situation in their journey. In other words, they have mastered each and every plateau. When you get advice from an expert who has done what you are trying to do they can tell you what action is best to break through your current plateau. They have discovered how to break through the plateau phases they have experienced and you can save time and resources by learning from the experts.

Never discount the hard work done by people who have persevered through the peaks and valleys of their journey by calling them "talented" and assuming that their success has come easily for them. Not only does this create a limiting belief for yourself, that achieving your dreams requires something you do not possess, but also you accept the fact that things must come easily for you and you have no business chasing that particular dream. If you follow in the footsteps of an expert who has already walked the same journey you are on towards success then you will be able to reproduce their results by reproducing their plan. The only difference is that an expert will not panic when things become hard or when you are not moving in the right direction. You might panic however, because you have not been at the same level long enough to know how to make minor adjustments and appear calm and collected. In other words, you may look like you are riding your bike for the first time all over again, over-correcting and crashing as you make your way through your personal success journey.

By the way, one key to success is to fail faster than anyone else you know! The more you fail the more experience you will have.

Successful people fail and instead of sitting in their failure and feeling sorry and pity for themselves, they get back up and look for the next opportunity to try again. Maybe even try again using a different strategy.

WATCH OUT FOR IMPOSTERS

While learning from experts is a fantastic idea to help speed up the time between the journey and the realization of success you must be diligent in identifying imposter experts. These people might be the physical trainer who is overweight, the financial advisor who is broke or the divorced marriage counselor. These people are to be avoided at all costs.

As Jim Rohn so beautifully says, "stand guard at the door of your mind." You must always be in charge of who you take advice from and what you allow to enter your mind.

As we discovered through the last few chapters, your mindset has everything to do with your success or your failure. The moral of these chapters is that you must welcome failure to succeed and when you hit a plateau, accept it.

As a matter of fact, when you hit a plateau you need to learn to get excited about it. Tell yourself, "Yes!!! Here is the plateau and an opportunity for profound wisdom and growth, what will I learn from it?" Or, "What do I need to learn to reach the next level?", "How will this breakthrough set me apart from the masses?" Always remember, progress is never linear.

Happy Plateau!

Bonus Material
Diagram on how DIP and progress work.

Download:
www.LivingImpossibleDreams.com/bonus/dip

DIP

CHAPTER
10

TALENT IS OVERRATED

"Effort, hard work, attitude, preparation, attendance, working harder than others and being coachable all have one thing in common... they require zero talent!"

- Freddy Behin

Competency and mastery is simply a matter of skill set and a matter of how well you control your skill set to produce results in a consistent manner. Skill sets are attainable and skill sets are just a process. Everyone who has a skill set had to develop it by doing it in a consistent manner. The skill may have happened by accident at some point, but in order to produce it reliably and consistently, work and time had to be spent on it. We believe that talented people have a certain predisposition with some skills they have. When we think about talent we believe that it is a fact and/or a god given gift.

We think you either have it and are blessed or you are lacking in and therefore you appear unlucky.

However if you view talent as a measurement of skill set and how it relates to time, you realize that it is just a measuring point and not an indicator for success.

The relationship of your skill set to the time it takes you to master it is what we call talent. Talent is when the mastery can be achieved faster. An athlete who qualifies for the Olympics on his first attempt versus another athlete who makes it to the subsequent Olympics are both still Olympians and they have both reached the same goal. However the first athlete may seem more talented since he achieved the results earlier. In other words the second athlete had to still master certain skill sets before he was ready to deliver the consistency that the first athlete demonstrated. Same level of mastery just a bit later in the timeline.

When you have the ability and skill set to do something or learn and master something faster than the average then, you are labeled as talented. The key point here is that the skill set of the talented athlete eventually gets matched by the not so talented athlete and if the talented athlete has not continuously improved on his mastery he will be bypassed by the non talented athlete.

I have seen so many apparently talented gymnasts who get things fast at first get ran over by a gymnast who showed no talent at the beginning. The talented kid had a higher starting and entry point as the non-talented kid. But as the slower kid builds their skill sets, they will eventually reach the same entry point as the talented gymnast. It just took them some more time to get there.

Therefore where you start this journey is not an indicator of your success. You can enter the process at any point. Your entry point is an accumulation of your mindset, belief system and mastery of some basic components in other areas, which have given you the prerequisite to enter at a later stage of this process. It is not just a miracle but something that was developed.

For example if you are a high level athlete and you have already established strong physical proficiency in your sport, you will have a much higher entry point starting a new sport.

Therefore, talent is not a guarantee for success but a starting point on a time line. We label someone talented when they cover more ground at the beginning of their entry and journey. Regardless where your entry point is at, if you do not work on your skill sets you will not get to the mastery level and as time passes someone who started lower than you will pass you by.

The great news with this concept is that if you are willing to do the work and pay the price you will be able to acquire the skill set and remove the story about you not having talent and achieve success as well.

The truth is that, you can enter anywhere along your journey to success and work your way up to the achievement of the destination. However you must divorce your stories about limitations and talent. You must destroy your many stories about why you are disadvantaged. Is it true that in order for you to have a great relationship or to be happy that you will need a great deal of money or the perfect body? Is it true that in order to be successful in life you must have rich and successful parents? It is wrong to say to yourself that, "With those things I could have achieved anything. With those resources I could have attended a finer school and only then could I have landed the job or career I truly want. Then I would have achieved greatness." This is a very self-limiting thought pattern and it severely hinders your chances for success. Be very careful when you say to yourself, "If only I had...", "I wish I was...", "I wish I could..."

I truly believe that we set up these restrictions and lie to ourselves as a way to excuse our inability to achieve greatness in life. Somewhere along our path in life we decided that success must occur within a certain time-frame and that achieving what we desire exists on a timeline. If we do not reach success within a certain amount of time or within a certain amount of attempts then we think we will never attain it. We consider ourself as failure.

Many women believe that there is a certain point in life by which they must have attained a certain status. If you are not in a meaningful relationship, have not had enough commitment or have not gotten married and had children by a certain time, then you have failed and missed your chance for a meaningful and fulfilling relationship and it is now too late to achieve happiness.

Many men believe that when they reach a certain age there are certain accomplishments that they should have achieved such as the right job, career, house or car. We often place ourselves on a tight timeline.

The question is: Where do these timelines come from? Who makes these rules and does it even matter what age we accomplish greatness? Does it really matter when greatness is achieved? Is it not the journey that matters most in getting to where you want to be?

Would you be less successful if your goals were achieved in four years rather than two? How about in six years rather than three? Is an Olympian less impressive if they miss the Olympic team their first tryout but make it successfully on their second attempt? Is a doctor less of a skilled practitioner if they took an extra year or two to pass the board exams? Does marriage and your ability to be a good husband or wife diminish if you wait a few years later than imagined?

The simple answer is no. The timeline does not matter. When you achieve your personal goal is irrelevant to the fact that you moved forward in life and the goal was achieved.

By setting goals with an unrealistic timeline you are exposing yourself to the psychology of "I am not good enough," and as discussed prior, when you do not feel good about what you are doing, you stop taking action. The key is to understand that your belief in a timeline constraint forces you to not achieve your goals on time. The fact is that you must never give up on your goals. Period. The only time you can submit to defeat is when you give up. As long as you are moving towards your goals, even if it feel that you are not making any progress, you have a chance. As long as you are still in the game you have a chance.

Simply set a new date or create a new timeline for achievement. This is a simple psychological shift. Sadly, too many people have already decided to quit on themselves based on their blueprint of life on an unrealistic timeline.

CHAPTER 1

CHAPTER
11

CONCLUSION

What have you learned so far? Has my journey inspired you and informed you that an average person can indeed achieve greatness? If you have said, "Yeah, that is easy for you to say. You are the genius athlete who was born lucky" then you need to go reread the message in Chapter One because you probably missed the point.

On the other hand, if you realized that the success in different areas of your life has used the same formula or blueprint that I have just shared, that is great! If you have realized that the areas in your journey where you have failed has missed one or two points of the formula, find a coach or a mentor to help you break through that plateau.

At this point you must make the decision to either be the driver or the passenger for your life's journey while you pursue your happiness and *im*possible dreams. If you want to be the passenger, that will mean that life is happening to you and you will have little to do with the outcomes you experience. You will simply be on the ride with preset skills you can utilize; nothing more, nothing less. Anything above and beyond your preset programming would seem out of your reach.

For those who are driving their life however, they are fortunate enough to believe they are able to achieve greatness and will hone better skill sets to ensure that happens. Passengers of life must be okay with sitting idly by and accept whatever direction the drivers in life take them. This means accepting the times when life is "stuck in neutral" and you are not going anywhere towards your journey. This also means accepting the end result of life.

Not taking action is in and of itself, an action. It is the action of producing zero results. The only guaranteed results in life are when no action is taken.

The moment you change your decision and become the driver of your life is the moment that you regain control and are able to have purposeful and driven actions and outcomes. You will be able to live the life you truly want to live. These are the beginning actions that lead you to achieving your dreams.

All through this book it has been my intention to instill in you the desire for greatness. That desire for greatness is a skill set and therefore, something that can be learned. By learning to follow a certain process you prepare yourself for the journey to making *im*possible dreams a reality.

In review, we discussed in the Mindset Chapter that how you view yourself is the first and most important step in any process. You must visualize yourself succeeding. In order to complete any masterpiece painting the artist must first visualize the end result.

For any building to be constructed, the architect first visualizes every aspect of the building before it is built. Nobody starts creating foundations and puts in steel beams, wood and metal without a plan or vision. Just like homes, greatness requires a plan and a vision to be built.

If in your first step you have not had a visualization occur or your end result is unclear then you will not be able to achieve the outcome. Your first step is extremely important. The view of yourself and your abilities is vital to knowing your success level. See the outcome and achieve the goal in your mind before you take the next step.

All self-limiting beliefs must be eliminated for you to achieve your goals. Can you see what is holding you back from being victorious? When you answer these questions you will do whatever is necessary to resolve those issues.

If the answer is, "I am not strong enough," then the solution is to do whatever is necessary to become stronger.

If the answer is, "I am not educated enough" then do whatever it takes to become more educated. The truth is that whoever is succeeding in that field has done the work. If you are lacking, all you have to do is what they have done.

The first time you achieve something that you thought was impossible, a shift occurs within your mind.

That shift is in your belief that a possibility exists. It then becomes easier for you to do it again. That one simple shift can facilitate your ability to achieve more and more. What if you could create that mindset? What if the secret to getting more success out of life was to live it in your mind first and then take the appropriate actions as if success is guaranteed?

It is mandatory to train yourself to shut down your entire negative belief system even if some of those beliefs may be true. Repeating them to yourself will not help you, shut them down. The voices that constantly tell you about your fears and why you would fail have to be shut down. Put them on mute and if they still voice an opinion, acknowledge it and thank yourself for the feedback, but tell it that you are "going to do it anyway!"

There might be facts involved in these dissenting opinions. Still, you must stop thinking negative thoughts and focus on what IS possible and what CAN be achieved. Then begin imagining yourself succeeding and visualize yourself doing what it is you hope to achieve.

In the Desire chapter I discussed how your desire can affect your outcome. I have seen so many "talented gymnasts" come through my career with zero work ethic or a desire to practice hard. Repeatedly I have seen them get crushed by the so-called "non-talented gymnasts" because they are willing to put in the work and have the desire to make the extra effort. The concept of Desire is what sets people apart in their attitude towards success.

You must get excited about why you are doing the work. You have to be excited and motivated to take action. When you get excited about what you want to do then you will take more action and more easily discern what the right action is. When you take more action you will achieve better results. Better results facilitate the cycle of improvement and your journey continues. You will become more excited and more motivated and you will be rewarded for all the effort you have put in. Therefore you will continually take more action.

Without Desire even the best strategies will not work. You need a compelling "why", and specifically "why" your goal is a "must", instead of a "should" or just a dream and an intent. There is a big difference in how much effort you put on something when it is only a should. The power is always diminished to take action sometime in the future when you say: "I should go to the gym and exercise", "I should be getting back in shape", "I should be taking care of my finances", "I should be taking care of my relationship." But when you say "I must" you shift the power to now. It becomes an urgency. Not doing so will cause pain and will have consequences so you must do it now. The urgency of a must will give you leverage to take action now. Be clear of how this will change your life? It is a lack of Desire that has created impossibilities throughout all time for humanity. Conversely, all innovations and breakthroughs have come from the desire that the outcome is a must and there is no other option but to achieve the end result.

In the Decision Chapter we discussed that without making a Decision or being decisive you simply have a choice sitting on the shelf and hope. All you are actively doing is wishing, hoping, praying and dreaming that something good will happen. It is in this moment of your Decision that your guiding forces within you will point you in the direction of success. It is when you make a Decision that defeat is no longer an option. Only then will you do whatever it takes to achieve your *im*possible dream.

Perhaps making a Decision to wake up a couple of hours earlier every day to read a book and give yourself more knowledge or spend time with a mentor and ask questions that will be the help you need. Your moment of Decision, when you decide you are willing to do whatever it takes will provide the push you need to move forward through adversity. The moment when you become 100% committed to taking the steps and actions which lead to victory regardless of any obstacles that you take full responsibility for your actions and your dreams become within your reach.

Once you take total responsibility for everything that happens to you then there is no chance for blaming others or circumstances for your lack of success. Life is all about you and the actions you take which makes blaming others unrealistic. Leave all excuses and rationalizations out of your mindset. You are who you are, where you are and precisely what you are doing today and the results you are getting today is because of all the actions and inactions you have done in your past.

If you have financial success it is because of the decisions and responsibilities you have taken previously. If you are in a passionate relationship it is because of the decisions, actions and responsibilities you have taken in your relationship. If you are healthy and have a vibrant life it is because of those decisions you have taken to make it that way.

"You are where you are because of all the decisions you have made in the past for your life"

- Freddy Behin

I recently had a conversation with one of the parents of a boy on our gymnastics team. At a competition, his mother noticed that another child from another team was doing amazingly well and much better than her son. It was amazing to me that instead of looking at her child and taking responsibility she instead came up with excuses.

One of the excuses was that the other child was home-schooled and had more time at the gym and therefore was the better gymnast. Of course, the reality was that the other child did not have any extra gym time but instead had the same amount of time for training. The difference was what he did with the training time he was given. He was more focused and dedicated during training.

My response to this mother was to not discount the hard work that was done to achieve the success that this boy achieved. I said to her, "If we would have given your son double the time for training he would have done the same exact quality of workout and just doubled his workout time. He would not change what he had done. He would just increase his standing around time and not take any action due to fear and lack of responsibility." It therefore stands to reason that the other child having been home-schooled did not make any difference in his performance level. However, what did make a difference was his performance was the daily decisions to take responsibility for his actions.

What this mother needed to realize was that others were taking twice the amount of turns on the apparatus and her son was skipping turns which was holding him back. If he makes the choice that he will take every opportunity instead of skipping turns he is more likely to succeed. However, if he continues to skip turns and falls off the apparatus three out of every five attempts during practice then he will also fall three out of every five attempts during competition.

"If you kinda try, you will kinda get results."

- Freddy Behin

Her son's job was to increase his number of successful tries. In other words, take as many turns as possible and stop skipping turns during practice. That would indicate responsibility for his actions.

It takes an enormous amount of self-control to refrain from making excuses. It takes a tremendous amount of discipline and integrity to not blame something or someone else for our inability to succeed. It is this discipline of taking true responsibility for our actions and how we react that results in everything that we are, everything that we have, everything that we accomplish, and ultimately everything that we will accomplish. Even if you are not directly responsible for something that has happened to you or your situation you are still responsible for how you choose to deal with that situation or setback. What you say, think and do will directly influence your results.

> *"Everything that happens to you may not always be your own fault, but everything that happens to you is your responsibility!"*
>
> - Freddy Behin

You will get out of life exactly what you put into it. Never discount the effort of others who are great and the hard work they have put in to achieve their greatness. Never search for excuses or say, "I have failed because I did not have X, Y or Z." Or, "I have failed because I was never given a chance." Never search for excuses to justify failure.

Be the driver of your life and be the driving force for your success. Make the right decisions and always take responsibility.

In Planning Chapter we discussed the importance of starting with the end in mind and making out our journey. For any plan to work you have to have a clear vision of your outcome and define the end result. Find multiple ways of achieving that outcome and decide which strategy will be the most efficient way to get to your outcome. Have backup plans to know what to do when one strategy fails or hits a bump in the road.

The best way to plan is to observe others who are living the life you desire to live and achieving the outcomes you desire to achieve. Observe others who have consistently produced the same successful results repeatedly. If you wish to model them then observe what they do. What is their ritual? Remember that quite often they are the humblest people and some of the most approachable. You can talk to them and learn from them.

By directly talking with them through digital paths, social media, or even email, they will often be more than happy to share their secrets with you.

In this chapter we also talked about the importance of anticipating setbacks. Understanding when setbacks are normal and when they are not part of a normal process. By anticipating setbacks you prepare yourself to deal with them and still move towards your goal.

In Preparation Chapter we discussed how your psychology can be the reason for your success or failure. You must be aware of your belief system around the imaginary walls that limit your thinking and abilities to succeed. Success requires the ability to expand your mind to accept the one-in-a-million chance.

We learned to designing a clear path to your goal while observing your behavioral patterns. Understand what the triggers are that slow you down and hinder your progress while discovering a solution to avoid those triggers. Conversely, you must embrace those triggers that give you the right behavioral patterns and move you towards your goal.

In Work Chapter we talked about achieving a better positive outcome faster by putting in the right work and being efficient at the work that we do. Most of all, you must "stay in the game."

If you make careless actions that might cause you injury regardless of whether it is financial, psychological or relationship pain, or if you injure yourself physically; you will impede your progress.

I want to remind you that no secret or strategy alone can grant success. You still must have the right mindset, desire and ability to make a decision wholeheartedly.

Understanding the 80/20/1 rule is very important in keeping you from stopping your progress due to inefficiencies and feeling overwhelmed by too much on your plate. Remember to narrow down your options and to do lists to an orderly list. Order the list by items that will give you the most results. Continue this process until you find the one item that would be the most important item that will produce the most effective result. You start with that and only focus on that first. Once you complete that you should have started a momentum and then you can move to the next item in the list.

In this chapter we also reviewed the four levels of mastery and competency. Moving from an unconscious incompetent level where you lack the knowledge and skill set to the unconscious competent level where you have mastered the skill set so well that you can now perform it without thinking about it and it has become a "reflex" or a habit. The key aspect to remember here is that when you move to the second stage where you become conscious about the work you have to do to gain the skill set. This is when most people give up on their dreams because they believe the work ahead is too long and too vast and that they must be achieving the results in a short period of time. This is the step that defines your ability to succeed in any field.

In Evaluation Chapter we discussed your work and feedback process. Do not forget that progress is not linear. You must be ready for plateaus and valleys in your process. Remember that no one has achieved greatness in a straight line. Even Tiger Woods, one of the greatest golfers of all time, has hit a plateau and had to regress and determine how to perfect that ultimate stroke. When he did he learned a new skill set and a new way to accomplish his goal.

This regression caused him to drop out of the golf tournaments for a while. He dropped 20-30 places in the world standings and caused people to think. "Wow, his success was a fluke. That was just a lucky streak that he had for a while." Then, he came back after he had overcome that plateau and valley learning a new skill set and was again able to achieve greatness.

Since progress is never linear, always remember that when you hit a plateau it is time to observe. Observe for what needs to change. Always ask yourself: "What about my plan worked and what did not? What needs improvement?" Make the required changes and move forward. You can always consult with someone that can see what you are missing. Other people such as mentors can do that for you. It might even be the same mentor you have already chosen. The best in the world in any field have mentors and coaches to help them see the one thing they don't see. The importance of having someone that can push you is more evident when you recall that there is an invisible boundary of limiting beliefs that you may not be able to see yourself. A great coach and mentor will be able to get you to expand your belief system and boundaries. Of course you have to keep an eye out for the imposters.

If you do what you have always done you will achieve the results you have already achieved. To change the results you must change your actions. For change to occur, action must be taken; the right actions!

Lastly, we discussed how talent is overrated. The key takeaway from this segment was to recognize that talent is a term we place on someone's ability level that has a shorter development time line. We are obsessed with the time and results concept. The shorter the time in their achievement the more talented we label these individuals. Recall that the entry point into this process is not an indicator for success. Only consistency and the right work is an indicator for success.

It is truly my hope that this book has opened a window in your mind's eye and that you are more inspired to go out and reach your *im*possible dreams. These dreams might inspire you today or they might be dreams that you gave up on. I hope you can now see that there are no limits to what you can accomplish in life.

Your perceived limits are only the boundaries and limitations you have set for yourself. Every lie you have been told including that talent and/or resources are what get you to success are false. If you practice these seven steps in all areas of your life on a regular basis you will become addicted to success. You will become addicted to being the best you can be. Just like any exercise, muscles will grow and the exercise becomes easier over time. It just becomes a part of who you are and a standard that you live by.

So, ask yourself a few questions: What self-limiting beliefs must I let go of? What new belief systems must I adopt? Who are the voices telling me that things are impossible? How do I shut them down? What must the new voices tell me to do?

Do I need to acquire a new peer group that will hold me to a higher standard? What activities can I begin that excite me and make me desire success?

I encourage you to start painting a new picture for your life. Return to your journey without limitations. The gift of life is very precious and you have now been given an opportunity.

It is your responsibility to live life to the fullest. It is your responsibility to use your own gifts that have been given to you and use them to their fullest potential. It is time to step up and be the best you can be. Most importantly however, it is important to know that you have greatness inside of you.

How many lives will you be able to change by becoming the best that you can be? Whose life will you be able to touch or inspire?

It is also important to never stop dreaming. Now that you know you can live your *im*possible dream, start taking the right actions towards living it.

Congratulations! If you have read the book this far I have full confidence in you that you are a person of discipline and action. Honestly, this is not patronizing you because you are now amongst the top 5% of people who finish what they start. This means that you already have a great head start towards achieving your dreams!

Now that you have learned the principals in this book I want you to make sure you set clear deadlines for your outcomes. Go to my website to get more tools to guide you through this process.

If you are interested in having me come in and speak or consult for your company or you would like to hire me for yourself then please email me or go to:

www.FreddyBehin.com

Finally, if you enjoyed this book about my journey and my principals and believe that there is value in this book to enhance the lives of your employees, co-workers, clients, family, kids and friends, then I encourage you to get them to read this book and start changing their lives so they can live their *im*possible dreams.

Most importantly, be sure to let me know about your success stories! I would love to hear how you are implementing the strategies you have learned in this book.

Live to the fullest and live with love and compassion!

Time will not wait for you!

Bonus Material

Get all your dreams organized and create a plan to live ALL your Impossible Dreams.

Download:

www.LivingImpossibleDreams.com/bonus/mydreams

MY DREAMS

www.LivingImpossibleDreams.com
www.FreddyBehin.com

FREDDY BEHIN, MD

ABOUT THE AUTHOR

Most goal-driven achievers aspire to one day rise to the top. But, it's a rare few who rise to the top in more than one area. Dr. Freddy has risen to the top several times – and he's done it with heart.

Freddy Behin is a modern-day Renaissance Man - an international competitive gymnast turned, compassionate doctor, creative software developer, and a successful entrepreneur.

He is a Professional Speaker, #1 Bestselling Author, and a Peak Performance Life Coach.

As the founder and owner of a very large gymnastics facility and training center in California, Freddy has helped over 9000 children enjoy the experiences and challenges of gymnastics. For over 20 years, his commitment to his community's youth has helped build a foundation for strong, confident young adults.

Beyond his local community, Freddy also donates his time, money and surgical skills to change lives around the world through his philanthropic work. His mission is to make a difference and instill hope in people around the world. With an intimate small group of like minded individuals Freddy strives to save and transform lives.

Freddy's true passion is helping his clients achieve greatness. As a top Peak Performance Coach, Freddy's expertise is in guiding top business leaders and professionals to higher levels of success and fulfillment.

Freddy's diverse background has taught him how to rise above any and all challenges he has experienced. He developed a signature system to maximize potential and target specific areas that his clients want to overcome, change or take to a higher level in their business and personal life.

Freddy operates from the heart and is an inspirer and sculptor of souls. He creates happiness and delivers results for people he comes in contact with.

Freddy has a diverse level of interest and when he is not changing lives he enjoys playing bass guitar in his studio with amazing musicians or local scenes to entertain people. He has always been fascinated by magic and as a new hobby and as someone who practices his own teachings, he has become a member of the Academy of Magical Arts in Los Angeles and hoping to perform one day at the Magic Castle as a professional magician.

Freddy lives his life with passion and gives everything he choses to do his full effort.

If you've ever felt that you were meant for more. If you've ever felt like there was more of you waiting to be fully expressed.

If you've ever felt like you could achieve more, or wanted to achieve impossible dreams yourself, you must contact Freddy!

Don't waste any time, start yourself on the path of achieving your own impossible dreams today! Freddy would be honored to be your guide!

Contact us if you are interested in having Dr. Freddy Behin speak to your organization and inspire, motivate, entertain, and educate your people.

You may be a candidate to be coached personally by Freddy if you would like to achieve higher fulfillment and success in your life. He will help you take your emotions, health, finances, business, and relationship to the next level.

www.FreddyBehin.com

NOTES

NOTES